45 Law School Recommendation Letters That Made a Difference

Dr. Nancy L. Nolan

Copyright 2010. Nancy L. Nolan, Ph.D.

All rights reserved. No part of this book may be reproduced or transmitted in any form or by any means, electronic or mechanical, including photocopying, recording or by any information storage and retrieval system without written permission from the author, except for the inclusion of brief quotations in a review.

Electronic, CD-ROM, and paperback versions published by:

Magnificent Milestones, Inc.
www.ivyleagueadmission.com

13-digit ISBN: 9781933819501

Disclaimers:

(1) This book was written as a guide; it does not claim to be the definitive word on the subject of recommendation letters. The opinions expressed are the personal observations of the author based on her own experiences. They are not intended to prejudice any party. Accordingly, the author and publisher do not accept any liability or responsibility for any loss or damage that have been caused, or alleged to have been caused, through the use of information in this book.

(2) Admission to law school depends on several factors in addition to a candidate's reference letters (including GPA, LSAT scores, work experience and personal statement). The author and publisher cannot guarantee that any applicant will be admitted to any specific school or program if (s)he follows the information in this book.

(3) The letters in this publication are actual recommendations that were written on behalf of successful law school candidates. To protect the privacy of the writer and applicant, the names of all people, classes, schools, places, and companies have been changed.

Dedication

For students everywhere;
may the size of your dreams be exceeded only
by your tenacity to attain them.

Acknowledgements

I am deeply indebted to the students, professors, attorneys, and admissions officers who have shared their perceptions and frustrations about recommendation letters. This book, which was written on your behalf, would not be nearly as powerful without your generous and insightful input.

I also want to thank my colleagues at www.ivyleagueadmission.com for providing a constant source of support, along with the best editorial help in the business.

45 Law School Recommendation Letters That Made a Difference

Chapter 1:	How Academic References / Recommendations Are Used	8
	What Makes a Great Letter	8
	How Reference Letters are Used	9
Chapter 2:	Who Should Write Your References	10
	Academic References	10
	Letters from Undergraduate Committees	11
	Additional Reference Letters	11
	Red Flags Regarding Your Choice of Reference Letter Writers	12
	Challenges to Getting a Great Letter	13
Chapter 3:	Using the Rating Scale as a Guide	14
	Sample Rating Sheet	15
	Universal Traits that Law Schools Seek	16
Chapter 4:	How to Ask for a Reference	17
Chapter 5:	How to Write a Persuasive Reference Letter	20
	Organizing the Letter	20
	Writing Guidelines	21
	Explaining Weaknesses	22
	Common Problems In Reference Letters	24
	Helpful Phrases for Reference Letters	24
	General Traits To Emphasize	27
Chapter 6:	Letters from Professors	28
Chapter 7:	Letters from Employers / Supervisors	35
Chapter 8:	Letters from Co-Workers, Clients & Peers	42
Chapter 9:	Letters that Document a Candidate's Volunteer Work	50
Chapter 10:	Letters for Candidates with Advanced Degrees	56
Chapter 11:	Letters for Older and Non Traditional Candidates	62
Chapter 12:	Letters that Explain a Gap on a Candidate's Resume	67
Chapter 13:	Letters that Document an Adversity	72
Chapter 14:	Letters that Explain Low Grades or LSAT Scores	77
Chapter 15:	Hall of Shame: References That Do NOT Open Doors	82
Summary		85

Appendices 86

Appendix 1:	College Dean's Evaluation Form	87
Appendix 2:	Request for Reference Letters	88
Appendix 3:	Sample Rating Sheet	89
Appendix 4:	Sample Match Points	90
Appendix 5:	Sample Thank You Note for a Reference Letter	91
Appendix 6:	Reference Letter Request Form	92

45 Law School Recommendation Letters That Made a Difference

Chapter 1: How Academic References / Recommendations are Used

For most candidates, few experiences are as daunting as applying for admission to law school. Competition is fierce at top US programs, where candidates search for every viable way to differentiate themselves. Ironically, in their zeal to make the best possible impression on the admissions committee, most candidates tend to overlook one of the most important aspects of the application: their reference letters.

Although academic achievements are important, they are only a small part of the admissions decision. Increasingly, top schools are placing greater weight on the quality and depth of your recommendations. As admissions officers, it is their responsibility to admit talented, multi-dimensional people with the potential to succeed in the legal profession. Ultimately, that requires evaluating not just a candidate's intellectual ability, but other traits that are not reflected by grades and test scores.

As a result, reference letters from credible third-party sources who can objectively evaluate your integrity and character are paramount in the evaluation process. In fact, they often play a key role in whether you are offered a seat in the class.

From our perspective, candidates don't place much emphasis on their letters of reference for two reasons:

1. they don't think they can control their contents
2. they don't know the specific steps they should take to improve their recommendations

This publication offers a viable plan for getting reference letters that convey *exactly* the attributes you want the admissions committee to see.

From our perspective, smart candidates give their reference letters that same level of attention that they give to their personal statements. They take the time to find the *right* people to say the *right* things in the *right* level of detail. In a highly competitive applicant pool, the choice between two equally qualified candidates often comes down to the quality and depth of their recommendations. Choosing the wrong people to write your letters can have devastating consequences.

Sadly, most recommendations we see are short, vague and non-persuasive; they do little to convince us that the candidate is special enough to earn our support. Getting great letters requires planning, hard work and initiative, but is well worth the trouble.

What Makes a Great Letter?

A great letter supplements the data you have provided the school about your academic and professional history with independent corroboration of your performance and potential. It also provides critical information about your personality, ethics and integrity that isn't captured anywhere elsewhere in the application. The BEST references are short, specific and insightful. They are written by faculty members and seasoned professionals who know you well enough to share specific examples of your best traits.

Here is what the committee hopes to learn from your reference letters:

   a. Your specific qualifications, including the depth of your academic and professional experiences
   b. Your unique traits that aren't covered anywhere else in the application
   c. Your demonstrated commitment to pursuing a legal career
   d. How you compare to other candidates with similar aspirations

From our experience, reference letters are the ONLY reliable indicator of several essential character traits, such as humor, maturity and tenacity. Many candidates write compelling essays to convince us that they are smart, funny team players, but it carries FAR more weight if an objective third-party confirms that. A thoughtful, well-written reference letter, which includes specific *examples* of a candidate's strengths, can make or break an application.

How Reference Letters are Used

As a general rule, recommendation letters supplement the primary admissions criteria for law school, which are your GPA and LSAT scores. In highly competitive programs, the applicant pool can quickly be sorted into three categories:

a. candidates with excellent grades and LSAT scores: good chance of admission
b. candidates who are borderline cases: application is competitive, but not outstanding
c. candidates with low grades and disappointing LSAT scores: poor chance of admission

Unfortunately, if you fall into category c, even great letters of recommendation may not save you from rejection. Highly competitive schools often screen out weaker applicants by imposing a minimum "cutoff" for GPA and LSAT scores. Although a reference letter can "explain" a disappointing score, it usually cannot compensate for it. Top schools will only give so much leeway to candidates who do not present a solid track record of success.

In contrast, reference letters for candidates in category a are usually disaster checks. These applicants have exceptional grades, top test scores and impressive personal statements. On paper, they are everything a law school is looking for. Their reference letters must:

a. validate their success
b. document their character, integrity and work ethic

For candidates in category a (excellent grades and test scores), a bad or mediocre recommendation can be extremely harmful. If your reference letters cast doubt upon the positive picture you have created (or reveal a serious character defect), the committee will be less likely to take a chance on you.

Surprisingly, nearly 70% of the applicant pool falls into category b, or borderline. These candidates have competitive grades and LSAT scores, but are otherwise not distinguishable from others with similar "numbers." Their acceptance or rejection often hinges on an exceptional intrinsic quality that captures the committees' interest and makes a positive impression. In some cases, this can be their commitment to family, their dedication to community service or their ability to overcome an obstacle. Reference letters from third parties who can document these activities can make or break their applications.

Chapter 2: Who Should Write Your References

Before you ask anyone to write a letter for you, carefully review the instructions from each school where you plan to apply. From our experience, each school takes a slightly different approach to the recommendation process. Some accept free-style letters, while others expect the reviewer to complete a rating form that includes a dozen different attributes. Some schools specify who should (and should not) write your letters, while others leave the choice up to you.

Schools also differ in the number of letters they require (and accept), with most requiring at least two (and accepting no more than five). Follow each school's instructions *exactly*, regardless of how much it complicates the process on your end. Remember, this is the school's first chance to evaluate how well you follow instructions; it's not the time to be a rebel.

As a general rule, schools expect to see reference letters from the following people:

1. Your undergraduate committee or adviser
2. A professor from your major field of study
3. Your major professor, if you are a graduate student
4. Your research advisor, if you have conducted academic research
5. Your supervisor, if you are currently employed

In many cases, the school's requirements will automatically determine who writes your letters. If so, approach each author with the information suggested in this publication to ensure that you get the best recommendations possible. On the other hand, if you have a choice of authors (or the luxury of submitting additional letters), try to pick the people who can best support your candidacy.

From an admissions perspective, a substantive letter of reference has three important features. The author:

a. understands the intellectual demands of law school
b. knows you well enough to evaluate your qualifications
c. is willing/able to provide enough supporting detail to justify his/her assessment

As a general rule, you should avoid sending letters from teaching assistants, friends, school alumni, relatives, clergymen or politicians, UNLESS they have personally supervised your academic or professional work and can comment on the specific attributes that are being evaluated in the admissions process. You'd be surprised how many people fall into this trap, not realizing that it actually hurts their chances. Every year, law schools receive letters from Senators, Governors and famous Hollywood stars in support of candidates they barely know. They are not impressed. Law school admission is serious business, not a popularity contest. The committee members are not so star struck that they will give a seat to someone just because her aunt works for the Governor.

Many candidates are surprised that letters from Teaching Assistants and Research Assistants carry little or no weight. From an admissions perspective, TAs and RAs are simply not knowledgeable enough about the selection process to be reliable sources of information. Law schools are looking for an honest appraisal of your character from people with extensive experience in the field. In academia, this is the tenured faculty.

Academic References

Surprisingly, even the best students sometimes have trouble producing exceptional letters of reference. Getting great letters requires a considerable amount of planning, particularly in the following situations:

a. At large universities, many classes are taught in large lecture halls that hold hundreds of students. Even if you ace the class, the professor may not know you well enough on a personal level to make an honest assessment of your suitability for law school.

b. Older applicants are at a disadvantage if an extended period of time has elapsed since they received their undergraduate degrees. Even the best professors can forget individual students after an extended period of time.

If you are still an undergraduate student, here are a few tips to help you stand out in the crowd:

a. Get to know your professors
b. Sit in the front row and ask questions during class
c. Try to take an upper-division class with a professor you particularly enjoy
d. Arrange to do a research project with your favorite professor during your sophomore or junior year

If you have already graduated, keep in touch with your favorite undergraduate faculty members via email and holiday cards. Later, when you ask for a letter of reference, they will be up to speed on your post-collegiate accomplishments.

Letters From Undergraduate Committees

A primary function of pre-law advisors at undergraduate schools is to evaluate and write reference letters for their students who wish to pursue graduate programs in the law. Most advisors will write letters for all students who request them, while some will only recommend students with a minimum GPA. Increasingly, law schools have expressed a preference for a letter from the *entire committee*, rather than just one advisor. In these cases, the letter is actually a composite recommendation that includes input from faculty members from different departments.

Prior to writing a reference letter, a committee member will interview you and determine whether your undergraduate performance and activities are consistent with the requirements for the law schools you are targeting. At many interviews, the committee will also probe your motivation for choosing this particular career. The subsequent letter will provide an overall assessment of you in comparison to other candidates from the same school.

From an admissions perspective, this letter is extremely important because it includes objective evaluations from individuals who are experienced in judging undergraduates who are applying to specific law schools. It is also perceived as being less biased than other letters. Although students can choose the authors of their other reference letters, they cannot choose (or otherwise influence) their entire undergraduate committee. As a result, their letters are considered to be more critical and objective than those solicited by the student directly. In borderline cases, they can make or break an application.

Increasingly, committees don't write formal letters, but send a standard evaluation form that rates each student on a variety of factors. If your school simply sends a rating form, I strongly encourage you to send additional letters of reference to support your application. The committee needs to read personal feedback from someone who knows your personality, communication skills and professional track record. A personalized letter that cites specific anecdotes and examples will highlight your strengths and set you apart from the crowd.

When you request your letter, solicit as much information as possible about the law schools that interest you. Many faculty advisors in the humanities are members of the National Association of Pre-Law Advisors, which offers a wealth of information on various aspects of the law school admission process. In addition to writing a recommendation for you, your pre-law advisor can be a great source of information for you on acceptance rates, qualifications and deadlines in the application process. If your university has a strong pre-law department, consider them your first stop for assistance and information.

In addition to traditional reference letters, *some* ABA-accredited law schools also require applicants to submit a form from the Dean of Students at their current school. The form's only function is to elicit negative information from the college's files that may not otherwise turn up in the law school application. The Dean himself must fill out the form, even if (s)he does not personally know the candidate.

If you have any questionable information in your college file, the Dean WILL report it on this form. This is how law schools usually find out about Honor Code violations, cheating rings and other issues of campus unrest. If a school you are applying to requires this form, make sure you know all of the information that is being reported on it. Immoral, illegal and unethical events in your past will usually eliminate you from further consideration. A sample copy of a College Dean's Evaluation Form is presented in Appendix 1.

Additional Reference Letters

In addition to a letter from your undergraduate committee or department head, you will also want to provide letters from other people to support your candidacy. The best reference letters are from credible sources that can reinforce and complement the information on your resume. Your authors should:

a. be successful leaders, researchers or scholars
b. have worked closely with you in school or in a professional environment
c. regard you as a talented candidate with incredible potential
d. have sterling academic and professional reputations

Furthermore, these authors must be willing to state that they:

a. know you well enough to evaluate your suitability for a legal career
b. have observed your growth and development over time
c. believe that you compare favorably to other candidates they have observed

From our experience, the strongest letters come from the following authors:

a. *Senior faculty members* with whom you have worked on a project. Try to get a letter from someone in your undergraduate major and another from a faculty member in a non-related field. You want to show the committee that you are a well-balanced person with strengths in diverse academic areas.

b. A *mentor* in your professional field, particularly if you have worked with this person for several years. Ideally, the author is a leader who can personally attest to your work style, personality and stamina.

c. A *supervisor from your participation in volunteer work or community service.* A well-crafted reference letter from an administrator of a non-profit organization who can personally attest to your devotion to an outside cause is highly perceived in the admissions process. The letter should cite the specific contributions you have made to the organization and your ability to get along with different types of people. These references, if chosen wisely, can make your application unique and memorable. They can also document how you have used your skills in an altruistic manner.

d. Your *boss or supervisor*, if you are currently working full-time. For older candidates, this is your chance to update the committee on what you have accomplished since you graduated from college. In most cases, there is a large difference in maturity between a 22-year-old recent graduate and a 27-year-old with several years of experience. Your reference letter from your employer should explain the type and extent of your professional experiences and how they have influenced your goals. Your supervisor can give the committee a first-hand account of your career progression, including the cultivation of previously unknown talents and skills.

Red Flags Regarding Your Choice of Reference Letter Writers

For what it's worth, here are the most common "red flags" regarding reference letters:

a. A candidate from an undergraduate school with a strong pre-law committee fails to have them send a reference letter. Many law schools will call the undergraduate institution to find out why.

b. A candidate has extensive professional experience, but does not offer a reference letter from his/her current employer. We understand that many candidates cannot risk their jobs by sending a letter from their immediate supervisor. In many firms, once your boss knows that you plan to resign to attend law school, your professional options will be limited. Law schools "get" that. If you cannot provide a letter from your boss without jeopardizing your job, you should submit a letter from a client or peer, rather than a supervisor. But you MUST send a letter from someone who can document your performance in your most recent position. If you don't, the committee will wonder what you are trying to hide.

c. A candidate who refuses to waive his right to see his reference letters. In the business world, reference letters are not cloaked in the same level of secrecy as in academia. In fact, most employers will give a candidate a copy of the recommendation as a matter of professional courtesy. If your authors extend this courtesy to you, that's terrific; you will know upfront what they have told the admissions committee about you. But don't insist upon seeing the letter if the author does not offer to show it to you. As a general rule, the admissions committee will view the letter as more forthcoming if you have waived your right to see it.

Challenges to Getting a Great Reference

Even the best candidates have trouble getting great letters. Here are the most common challenges, which we will address later in this publication:

1. Well-intentioned bosses and faculty members who don't know what to say. A great letter offers a critical analysis of your strengths and weaknesses from someone who knows you well enough to make an impartial assessment. The details must reinforce and complement the information in the rest of your application. In selecting your reference writers, you must make sure that they:

a. are good writers
b. know what to say
c. support you without reservation

Be VERY selective in who you ask.

2. Authors whose native language is not English. The best references discuss subtle nuances of a candidate's personality and professional skills, which requires a strong proficiency in written English. Authors who are uncomfortable with the language tend to write less, which ultimately hurts the candidate.

3. Faculty references who don't understand the non-academic aspects of the selection process. Top-tier law schools attract candidates from disciplines as diverse as art history and geophysics. To gain admission to these programs, applicants must demonstrate specific skills that are beyond the scope of their undergraduate course work. From our experience, many faculty references simply say, "Sam's academic record speaks for itself." Unfortunately, this is not helpful for highly competitive programs, where leadership and interpersonal skills are as highly valued as academic success.

4. Harried bosses and faculty members who don't have the time to write the letters for you. Rather than decline, they do a haphazard job, which does not enhance your candidacy.

5. Employers who refuse to offer any information beyond your title, salary and dates of employment. For legal reasons, many companies have taken a hands-off approach regarding recommendations; they either refuse all requests or limit their comments to names, dates and titles. Some firms even insist that all letters sent out on their corporate stationary be approved by a manager in human resources, who may not even know you. When you approach someone about writing a letter, don't automatically assume that (s)he has free reign to use his/her corporate logo however (s)he chooses. Company rules may severely restrict what current employees are allowed to say. Make sure that the person you have selected is free to write the type of detailed, enthusiastic endorsement that you need. If not, ask someone else.

6. Authors who instruct the candidate to write his/her OWN letter, which they agree to sign. This is a candidate's dream, until (s)he sits down to write. Sadly, most applicants lack the experience to assume the perspective and tone of someone in the recommender's position. They also don't really know what the committee expects. After viewing thousands of references, the committee has an excellent feel for authenticity. Most letters written by the actual candidates are embarrassingly easy to spot (and they are the kiss of death for the applicant's admission chances).

Fortunately, there are ways to tackle each of these challenges and get the letters you deserve. Read on!

Chapter 3:   Using the Rating Scale as a Guide

In most cases, each law school will provide its own evaluation form for your reference writers to complete. Although all forms are somewhat different, the one shown on the next page (and in Appendix 3) is a fairly representative sample, which we will use for discussion purposes in this publication. Before you ask *anyone* to write a letter on your behalf, take a look at the evaluation form that each school expects him/her to complete. Study the list of attributes that the writer must assess.

On our sample form, the attributes easily consolidate into four distinct categories:

1. **Academic Ability**:   intellectual curiosity, scholarship

2. **Motivation**:   reliability, perseverance

3. **Professional Strengths**:   judgment, resourcefulness, communication skills

4. **Personal Strengths**:   interpersonal relations, emotional stability, self-confidence, empathy, maturity

Note that only a few categories involve your GPA or academic performance. Even fewer relate to your mastery of any specific subject matter. Instead, the attributes are *intrinsic character traits* that govern your behavior in all aspects of your life. The BEST letters will come from people who are willing and able to discuss these traits in detail.

Before you ask someone to write a reference letter, take a few moments to list the ways that you have exemplified the traits on the rating scale. Restrict your observations to achievements and activities that your author *has actually observed*. Next, for each trait that you have selected, provide a specific example. These observations, which we will call your "**Match Points**," will form the foundation of your reference letter.

Sample List of **Match Points**   (for Dr. Martin's letter)

1. **Scholarship**:   completed three of Dr. Martin's psychology classes with an A grade. Completed my BA in Psychology with a perfect 4.0 GPA.

2. **Communication skills**:   excellent speaker and writer;   my oral presentation at the 2004 Annual Meeting of the American Psychological Association won third place in the national competition.

3. **Empathy**:   high emotional intelligence;   assumed workload for a fellow student after a debilitating car accident. Visited the student often during her medical leave and provided a consistent source of emotional support.

4. **Language Skills**:   fluent in English, Spanish and Russian; frequently translate documents and journal articles for the head of the psychology department.

5. **Motivation**:   assumed leadership responsibilities in the lab, including the supervision of two lab assistants. With their support, I completed a side project that yielded two publications in the *Journal of Adolescent Psychology*.

We will discuss this list further in Chapter 4.

Sample Rating Sheet

Factors: For each factor below, please indicate your opinion of this applicant's rating on that factor relative to other candidates you have observed.

Ranking Standards:

1. Exceptional, top 5%
2. Excellent, next 10%
3. Good, next 20%
4. Average, middle 30%
5. Reservation, next 30%
6. Poor, low 5%
7. No basis for judgment

Factors:

_____ **Emotional Stability:** Exhibits stable moods; performs under pressure

_____ **Interpersonal Relations:** Rapport with others; cooperation, attitude toward supervisors

_____ **Judgment:** Ability to analyze problems, common sense; decisiveness

_____ **Resourcefulness:** Originality; initiative, management of resources and time

_____ **Reliability:** Dependability; sense of responsibility, promptness; conscientiousness

_____ **Perseverance:** Stamina; endurance, psychological strength

_____ **Communication skills:** Clarity in writing and speech

_____ **Self-confidence:** Assuredness; awareness of strengths & weaknesses

_____ **Empathy:** Consideration; tact; sensitivity to the needs of others

_____ **Maturity:** Personal development; social awareness, ability to cope with life situations

_____ **Intellectual curiosity:** Desire to learn and extend beyond expectations

_____ **Scholarship:** Ability to learn, quality of study habits, native intellectual ability

_____ **Motivation:** Depth of commitment; intensity; sincerity of career choice

Evaluation Summary:

Compared to other law school applicants you know, please provide an overall evaluation of this candidate:

( ) Exceptional candidate, top 5%
( ) Excellent candidate, next 10%
( ) Good candidate, next 20%
( ) Average candidate, middle 30%
( ) Weak candidate, bottom 35%
( ) No basis for judgment

Universal Traits that Law Schools Seek

If at all possible, have your reference letters validate the following universal strengths, which are essential in a legal career:

Exceptional language skills. Write and speak clearly and concisely. Can argue both sides of a position with passion and intelligence. Responds to questions (and dissenting opinions) with confidence and grace. Excellent listing skills - can pick up subtle distinctions in discussions and debates.

Excellent analytical skills. Can make decisions that require the use of various types of reasoning. Can think independently, identify the essential point of a case or argument, and distinguish relevant details from extraneous information. These skills are often honed in science, mathematics, logic, and economics classes, which require the integration of data from multiple – and often conflicting –sources.

Thinks "outside the box." In emergency situations, there are rarely hard-and-fast rules to guide a person's judgment. Successful candidates can tolerate this ambiguity and recognize the exceptions that modify general rules. Law schools need to know whether an applicant is likely to be stimulated (or frustrated) by questions (and scenarios) that have no "correct" answers.

Thrives in a rigorous, interactive environment. Candidates who enjoy rigorous discussions and collaborative projects are more likely to flourish in the competitive atmosphere of law school. Additionally, students must be diligent and well-organized to keep pace with the amount of reading and memorization that law school requires. A mature attitude and healthy sense of humor are highly prized in the selection process.

Chapter 4: How to Ask for a Reference Letter

Once you have chosen your potential reference writers, you need to ask them if they are willing to tackle the job. Don't assume that every person you select has the time, energy or inclination to write a great letter of recommendation. Thankfully, by following these tips, you can maximize your chances of getting the *right* people to go to bat for you.

a. **Approach.** Don't simply call or send a form to your writers; always arrange for a personal meeting, if possible, or make a phone call to discuss your request (if the writer is not geographically close). Explain your desire to attend law school and your need for a comprehensive letter of reference. Discuss any issues or concerns the person has about your candidacy.

Verify orally that (s)he is willing to write a "strong letter of support," not just an average or lukewarm one. If the person declines, do not push the issue. If you sense any hesitation, graciously withdraw the request. You are better off asking someone else who can recommend you without reservation.

A face-to-face meeting also gives the writer an opportunity to ask clarifying questions. For example, which letters are mailed directly to the law school and which letters are returned to the student? Which envelopes must have the professor's signature on the seal? When is each letter due? By discussing these requirements with your writers in person, you can ensure that your letters arrive at the right place by the stipulated deadline.

During your initial conversation, feel free to mention the attributes you would like the letter to highlight; make sure that the person concurs with your own self-assessment. Although it is awkward (and somewhat embarrassing) to discuss your perceived flaws, it is *far* better to identify a non-supportive author now, rather than obtain a bad letter of recommendation.

b. **Documentation.** If the person agrees to write an enthusiastic letter, give him/her the following information:

  i. A cover letter with the names, addresses and deadlines for every letter you need   (Appendix 2)
  ii. The appropriate forms from each school that (s)he will need to complete
  iii. A summary of your "Match Points," which explain your fit for the program you have chosen   (Appendix 4)
  iv. A current copy of your resume
  v. Your personal statement
  vi. Pre-addressed, stamped envelopes for all letters

These documents will make the writer's job easier because they provide the relevant details for him/her to include in the letter. They will also set you apart from the crowd. In my career, I've written hundreds of letters of recommendation for students who were seeking jobs, advanced degrees, scholarships and fellowships. Only a small handful have ever provided this information, which is crucial for writing an effective letter. I am always impressed when a candidate takes the time to organize his/her needs and focus my energy in the right direction. By doing this, (s)he already demonstrates many of the skills that are necessary for success.

Increasingly, law school admissions committees expect writers to support the claims that they make in letters of recommendation. If a professor says "John is a persuasive speaker," (s)he must provide concrete evidence that John is actually a persuasive speaker. Unfortunately, few faculty members keep copies of student papers, quizzes or descriptions of a student's participation in the classroom. For this reason, you should customize the information on your Match Points for each individual author. Remind each person of your accomplishments in his/her class or department; include specific details. Don't assume that they have the documentation on hand to write a great letter.

A caveat for candidates who are still enrolled in their undergraduate studies; from my experience, many college seniors do not have a particularly well-organized resume. For academic references, make sure that your resume includes all of the information the author will need to draft a detailed letter. At the very least, please include:

a. your overall GPA
b. your major and minor
c. the titles and abstracts of any research papers you have written
d. honor societies to which you belong

- e. awards you have won
- f. activities in which you have participated (and any offices held)
- g. work experience
- h. service activities and volunteer work
- i. a description of your professional goals

By providing this information in a clear and concise format, you can help your authors make their best possible case for you.

c. **Timing.** Arrange for your reference letters no later than September in your senior year of college (for candidates who have already graduated, at least *six weeks* before you submit your application). Ideally, ask in the middle, rather than the end, of a semester. Usually, by semester's end, most professors are overwhelmed with requests for letters and yours will simply be another request in the pack. To increase your odds of receiving a more thorough recommendation, submit your request before the big rush.

Tell your reference writers all of the places you are applying at your initial meeting, so they can prepare all of the letters at the same time. Don't blindside them with requests for additional letters later on. From my experience, it's far easier to send out many letters at once than one or two at a time.

d. **Copy of the letter.** Without exception, you should waive the right to see all of your recommendations. Admissions committees place little stock in letters that the applicant insists upon seeing, because they know that the author is less forthcoming than if the reference was confidential. You may, however, ask the author to send a *copy* of the letter to you for your files. This is not a violation of the rules and gives you some assurance of the quality of your reference.

If a writer does not wish to provide you with a copy of the letter, don't insist upon it. Academic references are still mostly confidential, although the tide is turning very slowly towards full disclosure. This is a startling contrast to the business world, where copying the candidate on a letter of reference is standard practice and a professional courtesy.

e. **Format.** Letters from your professors should be professionally typed and printed on the school's stationary. Other letters you request may not automatically come in this form. If at all possible, ask your writers to send the letters typed on professional letterhead with a laser-jet or inkjet printer. For some law schools, the writers are not asked to submit a general letter, but to answer several specific questions. If this is the case, you should tailor your list of Match Points to address the specific questions that are asked by each school.

f. **Organization.** Organize the forms, envelopes, program descriptions, and other materials you will give to each reference writer in a logical manner. One simple technique is to paper-clip the form, program description, and the school's envelope together. Then, to make sure they remain together, place them in a large padded envelope; write your name, the writer's name and the date the letters are due on the outside of the padded envelope. Remember that you will have to create a separate padded envelope for each person who is writing a reference letter for you.

When you complete Appendix 2 (your request for reference letters), list the schools in chronological order, with the earliest deadlines first. The chronological list makes it easy for faculty members to complete your letters of recommendation on time.

g. **Follow-up.** Two weeks after a writer agrees to send the reference letter, verify that it has reached its destination. If it hasn't, ask him/her to send a second copy. Then, send a thank-you note to each person who took the time to write a letter on your behalf; it not only shows good manners, but will encourage the writer to continue to offer references for future applicants. A terrific example of a thank-you letter is included in Appendix 5.

Your final step, which is often overlooked by busy applicants, is to notify your authors of the final admissions decision. Use the opportunity to re-thank them for their continual support of your career. It is never too soon to build your professional network.

h. **If Asked to Write Your Own**. Increasingly, over the past several years, we have met many candidates whose busy bosses and professors were overwhelmed by the request to write letters of recommendation. The applicants were instead instructed to write the letter themselves and simply submit it to the "author" for a signature. Most applicants consider this a dream come true. After all, what could be better than a chance to "toot your own horn" under the guise of being your own boss or major professor?

Sadly, most candidates haven't a clue what an excellent reference letter looks like. To assume the perspective and tone of someone in your recommender's position requires a considerable amount of experience. Most letters written by the actual candidates are embarrassingly easy to spot: they include far too many details that a real reference letter wouldn't mention and they are identical in tone to the candidate's own writing.

We strongly discourage you from trying to write your own letters. Remember, the admissions committee has viewed thousands of letters and has a good eye for what a real recommendation does – and does NOT – say. There are also moral and ethical considerations with writing your own letters. Law schools do not want to admit sneaky candidates who bend the rules to suit their own whim; they want ethical candidates who are willing to obtain an honest appraisal of their credentials from an objective, well qualified third party. Instead of trying to write your own letters, give the author a copy of your Match Points (Appendix 4), which summarizes your fit for your program of choice. Ask him/her to elaborate on those points to complete the letter. If (s)he refuses, ask someone else, who is willing to take the time to write a reference that genuinely reflects your suitability for the program to which you are applying.

Chapter 5: How to Write a Persuasive Reference Letter

Assume for a moment that you've just been asked to write your first reference letter. If you are like most people, you were totally flattered by the request. After all, when a candidate asks you to recommend him/her for law school, it implies that you are an expert on the subject; you know what it takes to succeed in the legal profession. But that doesn't necessarily mean that you are in a position to endorse the particular candidate who has asked you. Before you agree to write a letter, you must have a frank discussion with the candidate about your ability to fulfill his/her expectations.

A. Establish honestly and directly whether or not you can write a positive letter on behalf of the applicant. If you only have limited knowledge of the person's talents (or a negative impression of him/her), then you cannot in good conscience provide a positive letter. From our experience, an ambiguous or lukewarm reference can cause as much harm as a negative one. Tell the candidate your concerns upfront. Although the conversation may be awkward, it will enable the applicant to address whatever issues you may have. Alternatively, the candidate may decide to pursue a more enthusiastic person to write a letter on his/her behalf.

Note: From our perspective, the most gracious ways to decline a request are to say that you:

1. do not have enough time to do an effective job
2. are not familiar enough with a candidate's work or background to do him/her justice
3. do not have the credibility to impress the committee at that particular school/program

In all cases, try to suggest someone else who can do a better job on the candidate's behalf. By keeping the emphasis on delivering the best letter possible, you can minimize any hurt feelings.

When deciding whether or not to write a letter, remember that your reputation is at stake. If you work in academia (and write numerous reference letters), admissions officers will eventually become familiar with what you have said about other candidates. If you routinely oversell the applicants (or over-inflate their capabilities), after a few years, no one will believe what you say. The best way to retain your credibility is to be highly selective in whom you choose to support. You will write fewer recommendations, but they will be more meaningful in the selection process.

B. If you agree to write a letter to support the candidate, you must maintain the integrity of the process by personally writing the letter, rather than simply signing a draft that the candidate has already written. However, soliciting ideas from the candidate regarding the focus and content of the letter is not only acceptable, but recommended.

C. Give the candidate a copy of **a Reference Letter Request Form** (Appendix 6), which summarizes all of the information you will need to write the letter. At the very least, you should have a copy of the candidate's:

1. Resume
2. Personal Statement
3. Statement of Goals
4. Match Points (Appendix 4)
5. Written permission for you to send a reference letter on his/her behalf
6. A complete list of all schools to which the letter should be sent, along with the deadlines for each

D. Before putting pen to paper, be sure to review your organization's policy regarding letters of recommendation. Since most letters are printed on corporate letterhead, many firms have rigid guidelines in place to protect themselves against potential lawsuits. The common rule is to write only positive, factual recommendation letters that refrain from any type of derogatory remarks. If you cannot adhere to this requirement, you should decline the candidate's request.

Organizing the Letter

As a general rule, reference letters include four distinct parts:

1. An **introduction**, which explains who you are, your relationship to the candidate and why you feel qualified to assess his/her suitability for the program. Explain how long you have known the applicant and in what capacity. State your qualifications for writing the recommendation letter. Why should the reader be interested in your perspective? How many other people of the applicant's caliber have you known; why does the applicant stand out?

2. A **discussion of the candidate's strengths** and how they relate to the needs of the program. Discuss the applicant's exceptional qualities and skills, especially those that are relevant in a legal career. As a first step, review the general categories of skills that we presented in Chapter 3. Include your own observations of the candidate's strengths, along with the list of Match Points that the candidate has provided. These observations will form the foundation of your reference letter.

We recommend that authors organize their discussion of the candidate's strengths in the following manner:

a. First, provide a *general assessment of the applicant's performance* and potential for career growth, in the context in which you know him/her. If the applicant was your student, mention how well (s)he did in your classes and the particular skills (s)he used to accomplish this. If the candidate is your employee, discuss how well (s)he executes his/her job responsibilities. Highlight the applicant's key accomplishments and strengths.

b. Next, discuss the candidate's *oral and written communication skills*. Highlight any publications or presentations you have observed.

c. Discuss the candidate's *maturity level and interpersonal skills*. Highlight exceptional personal strengths, including how well the candidate gets along with others and his/her level of reliability and responsibility.

d. Finally, discuss any *special skills or strengths* the candidate may possess, such as language fluencies, multicultural expertise or a commitment to volunteer work.

For each characteristic or trait that you mention, give specific examples or anecdotes to support what you say. In reference letters, the power is in the details; generalized praise is not particularly helpful.

3. A **comparison** of the candidate to others who have succeeded in law school. Give your judgment of the applicant, his/her qualifications and potential. Why should (s)he be considered over other candidates? How does (s)he compare to other law students you have known? Write only complimentary (yet factual) observations.

If asked to discuss a candidate's flaws or weaknesses, choose something that can be presented as an opportunity for growth (we offer several suggestions later in this chapter). The best choices are traits that the candidate has already taken steps to correct, such as a lack of knowledge or training in a particular area. Avoid unflattering or derogatory remarks.

4. A **conclusion**, which summarizes the candidate's outstanding strengths and abilities. Offer a strong ending, but don't overdo it. Excessive praise can be viewed as biased or insincere. Finally, list your contact information if you are willing to respond to follow-up correspondence.

Chapter 6 - 14 provide several samples of successful reference letters for law school, including letters that address special situations. They each use a different approach to convey the applicant's unique strengths. Use the letters as inspiration for your own original writing.

Writing Guidelines

1. As a rule of thumb, the "correct" length for a reference letter is one or two typewritten pages. You should include enough information to supplement the committee's impression of the candidate, without overwhelming the reader with details that are unrelated to the application.

2. Focus on qualitative information, rather than quantitative. By the time the admissions committee reads your letter, they will have already reviewed the candidate's transcripts and LSAT scores. Rather than repeat those details, you should share your "behind the scenes" insight into the candidate's performance and his/her potential to succeed in law school. To whatever extent possible, you should give the committee positive information about the candidate that they could not acquire any other way.

3. Read the candidate's personal statement to get an idea of the strengths that (s)he is trying to convey to the committee. Ideally, your letter will *complement* (and build upon) what the candidate has written in his/her personal statement without *duplicating* it.

4. Offer a balanced perspective of the candidate. Admissions committees appreciate letters that offer honest

assessments, including areas for growth; they do not expect perfection.

5. Do not make any statements that you cannot support with facts and examples. Do not editorialize or speculate. If you give an opinion, explain the incident or circumstances upon which you are basing it. Be able to document all of the information that you release. To avoid a possible claim of defamation, do not comment about the candidate's moral character.

6. Write with enthusiasm. Use powerful words, such as articulate, effective, intelligent, significant, creative, efficient, cooperative, assertive, dependable, mature and innovative. Avoid bland words such as nice, reasonable, decent, fairly and satisfactory. Although they may seem perfectly fine to you, in admissions circles, they scream "average" or "mediocre."

7. If there are extenuating circumstances that have impacted the candidate's academic or professional progress, you should obtain the candidate's written permission to disclose that information. Law schools value the perspective of someone who knows an applicant well, especially in reference to possible challenges that (s)he has overcome. Nevertheless, these topics (such as homelessness, divorce, or illness) should NOT be discussed in your letter without the candidate's express written permission.

8. Do **not** reveal any information that could be viewed as discriminatory, including the candidate's race, color, religion, national origin, political affiliation, age, disability, sexual orientation, physical appearance, citizenship status or marital status.

9. If you are an alumnus of the school to which the candidate is applying (or have completed a similar program), feel free to elaborate on the applicant's fit for that particular program. Explain how (s)he will add to the student body and be a good role model.

10. Type your letter on official letterhead and sign it in ink. A professional presentation will reflect positively on the candidate. Handwritten letters are not only difficult to read, but detract markedly from the writer's credibility. Sadly, admissions committees rarely take the time to read them.

11. If a candidate asks you to address a letter "to whom it may concern," note that in the body of the letter. Also note that the candidate has agreed to take responsibility for disseminating the letter to the proper person.

12. If your company has concerns about liability issues regarding reference letters, include the following sentence at the end of your letter:

"This information is provided at the request of [name of applicant], who has asked me to serve as a reference. My comments are confidential and should be treated as such. They reflect my own opinions about the candidate's suitability for law school. No other use or inference is intended."

This type of disclaimer explains the purpose of your letter and confirms that it was not written to hurt the applicant's reputation.

13. Ask the candidate to let you know the committee's decision.

14. Keep a copy of every letter you send – and document when you sent it. This information will come in handy if, for whatever reason, the letter does not reach its destination (and must be re-sent).

Explaining Weaknesses

For most authors, the trickiest part of writing a reference letter is discussing a candidate's "weaknesses" or "areas of development." Few writers want to document an applicant's faults on record, for both personal and legal reasons. Nevertheless, the BEST recommendations give a balanced perspective of the applicant, including a brief assessment of the areas in which (s)he can improve. If you omit this section, or offer an insincere reply, your letter will lose a portion of its integrity.

From our perspective, the best weaknesses to mention fall into three categories:

1. Areas that the candidate is already working on

Examples:

A poor public speaker who improves his/her skills by joining Toastmasters
Someone with no computer skills who takes a programming class
A candidate who joins a professional association to expand his/her network

2. Areas that will be addressed through the graduate program to which (s)he is applying

Examples:

A candidate with no international experience who applies to a program overseas
A successful paralegal who cannot advance in the profession without a law degree

3. Positive personality traits that need to be tempered

Examples:

A candidate who works 24/7, to the detriment of his/her personal life
A candidate who needs to reign in his/her sense of humor
A candidate who is overly detail oriented, but misses the big picture
A perfectionist who delivers top quality work, but takes forever to do it

Weaknesses that are Deal Breakers.

From our perspective, mentioning the following "weaknesses" will sabotage the candidate's application, and may leave the writer in a legal quagmire. In these situations, you should decline to write a reference on the person's behalf:

a. candidates who have committed immoral, illegal or unethical acts
b. candidates who cannot get along with other people
c. candidates who are incompetent in their current jobs
d. candidates with difficult personalities

No matter how clever you try to be, the committee will "read between the lines" to try to decipher what you AREN'T saying.

Examples: Sharon marches to her own beat, which few other students hear.
Because she is fiercely independent, Sharon excels at working alone.
Rather than participate in campus events, Sharon prefers to keep to herself.

Translation: Sharon is a misfit who is NOT a team player. She has low leadership potential.

Examples: In a few years, when he matures, Brad will undoubtedly fulfill his potential.
Regardless of the circumstances, Brad is always the life of the party.
After a slow start, Brad managed to complete his term paper.
Brad's speech, although short on content, was slick and polished.

Translation: Brad is a funny guy who is hopelessly immature. He's not ready for this commitment.

Common Problems in Reference Letters

Here are the most common problems we observe in reference letters. If at all possible, avoid sending letters that:

a. are typed on plain paper instead of letterhead.

b. do not include the writer's signature and/or contact information.

c. do not include the confidentiality waiver for the letter (sometimes, students forget to give the form to the writer; other times, the writer forgets to return the form to the school).

d. contain unsupported, over-enthusiastic or generic endorsements, instead of offering useful, balanced insights.

e. concentrate on the writer and/or the class, with only a brief reference to the student.

f. disclose personal and controversial information about the applicant that does not enhance his/her candidacy, including personal or political views.

g. contain school-specific or company-specific jargon that is unfamiliar to the admissions committee. If in doubt, show the material to an intelligent person whose formal education is in a different field. If (s)he cannot understand it, the committee probably won't, either. And, sad to say, they won't be impressed by something they can't understand.

Helpful Phrases for Reference Letters

Chapters 6 - 14 provide numerous examples of successful reference letters for law school. We encourage you to use them as inspiration for your own original writing. As you will see, there are several universal statements that are incumbent in all reference letters. If you aren't sure how to get started, or are struggling with writer's block, consider the following phrases as guidelines:

1. Opening Statements

I am writing this letter at the request of Jane Smith, who is an applicant for your entering law school class.

I am pleased to write this letter of recommendation for Jane Smith.

Please accept this letter as my enthusiastic endorsement of Jane Smith.

My name is Tom James and I am a Manager at Bank One. I am delighted to write a letter of reference for Jane Smith to support her application to law school.

2. Your Qualifications to Evaluate the Candidate

In my 20-year teaching career, I have advised approximately 450 students on independent research projects.

I have personally supervised ten interns every summer for the last five years as a trainer for Bank One.

In my career at Rice University, I have seen hundreds of undergraduate students seek admission to law school.

In over ten years as the CEO of Infotech, I have supervised 50 other programmers with Jane's education and experience.

3. How well you know the Candidate

I know Jane well, because she attended two of my sections every week, although only one was required.

Mark reported directly to me for two years prior to his well-deserved promotion to Manager at Bell South.

We enjoyed several after-class discussions about Jane's research, which offered fascinating preliminary results.

I was delighted when Rita asked me to be her advisor for her senior literature project.

4. Candidate's Greatest Strengths

Rachel has the rare blend of analytical and interpersonal skills that a legal career requires.

Rachel is the hardest working, most tenacious engineer I have ever known.

Rachel was one of the most productive, caring and effective nurses I have had the pleasure of knowing.

Rachel's greatest talent is fundraising on behalf of cancer research.

5. Assessment Statements

John is an enthusiastic self-starter with an impressive command of technology.

Despite the competing demands on her time, Alexis consistently produced high quality work in a timely fashion.

By using a highly creative approach, Carter quickly re-defined our expectations of a good project manager.

In his four years with us, Ben has completed four of my classes and has been one of our most successful undergraduate students.

6. Evidence to Support a Strength

Jake is the only student who came to all of my office hours to master financial theory. He was one of only two students to receive an A in the course.

Because of Jane's writing skills, I didn't hesitate to ask her to write a research report for a major policy decision. Based on Jane's sophisticated 20-page analysis of airborne contaminants, Congressman Jones lobbied the State for increased funding.

Jane's technological and quantitative skills are exemplary; the various scheduling, work-flow and asset management software systems that she developed contained complicated algorithms that are beyond the scope of most developers.

After the Supreme Court's examination of racial discrimination/affirmative action in law school admission at the University of Michigan, Fran produced a thorough and well-written analysis of the decision, arguing at length in support of Justice Clarence Thomas's dissenting opinion.

7. Rating or Ranking Statements

Jane was in the top 10% of her class.

Zachary has the best analytical skills of any chemist I have ever supervised.

Rachel is in the top 5% of all students I have seen, both in academic achievement and practical skills.

As a teacher, I treasure the rare student who has the talent and skill to make a significant contribution to his field. Zane is one of those rare students.

8. Mild Criticism / Presenting a Weakness

John's only fault is his retiring nature. His modesty sometimes hides his remarkable strengths.

Julie's persistence can turn into stubbornness, but her good nature ultimately prevails.

With training in finance, Carl will be better prepared to evaluate projects from a business perspective.

The only area of weakness that I ever noted in Jane's performance was her minimal background in statistics. Fortunately, she is now taking a class at the community college to remedy this deficiency.

9. Candidate's Potential for Success

I enthusiastically recommend David to your law school. This passionate, well-rounded student will be a fine attorney.

With her exceptional leadership, writing and quantitative skills, Sondra will be a credit to whatever law school she attends.

George's leadership potential in the legal profession is superb.

I feel quite confident that Joe will be an asset to both student life and academic excellence at Harvard Law School.

10. Closing Statements

I am pleased to recommend John for admission to law school.

Based on my time working with Susan, I recommend her very highly for a law school of Harvard's caliber.

In summary, I am pleased to recommend Jose without reservation.

From my observation, Zachary will undoubtedly succeed at whatever law school he chooses.

General Traits To Emphasize

Depending on your relationship with the candidate, the committee will have different expectations of what they expect your letter to say. As a general rule, these are the traits that are most highly prized in the admissions process.

Remember, when you draft your letter, you should restrict your comments to your actual interactions with the candidate – and the achievements *you have actually observed*. Anything that you've "heard" about the candidate from a third party, regardless of how flattering, will be regarded as hearsay if you repeat it in your recommendation letter.

Academic Strengths

- Intelligence
- Scholarship
- Analytical skills
- Reasoning skills
- Curiosity
- Mastery of specific subject area
- Innovative
- Insightful
- Creative
- Well-rounded
- Class participation
- Observant

Professional Strengths

- Leadership skills
- Hard-working
- Motivated
- Tenacious
- Ambitious
- Self-starter
- Creative
- Resourceful
- Efficient
- Good manager
- Writing skills
- Presentation skills
- Strong interpersonal skills
- Versatile
- Ethical
- Independent
- Well organized
- Planning skills
- Technical skills (be specific)
- Attention to detail
- High energy level
- Communication skills
- Attentive listener
- Perseverance
- Good judgment
- Negotiation skills

Personal / Interpersonal Strengths

- Friendly
- Optimistic
- Polite
- Well-mannered
- Mature
- Team player
- Patient
- Kind
- Empathetic
- Loyal
- Sincere
- Modest
- Sense of integrity
- Reliable
- Flexible
- Generous
- Assertive

Chapter 6: Letters from Professors

Nearly every law school requires candidates to send a recommendation letter from an undergraduate faculty member. Ideally, the author should be a full-time professor in a tenure-track position at his/her school, with one of the following titles/rankings: Assistant Professor, Associate Professor, Professor, or Dean.

If possible, avoid sending letters from teaching assistants, Ph.D. candidates, or adjunct faculty members, regardless of how enthusiastic they may be. From an admissions standpoint, authors in these positions do not have the perspective they need to compare you to other law school candidates. Consequently, their claims will not be given adequate weight in the decision-making process.

As we discussed in Chapter 2, the "perfect" professor to write your letter is someone who:

a. understands the intellectual demands of law school
b. knows you well enough to evaluate your qualifications
c. is willing/able to provide enough supporting detail to justify his/her assessment

In paragraph 1: the author should explain his/her relationship with you, including:

His/her title
How long (s)he has known you
How many classes you have completed with him/her
The titles of those classes
Any outside interactions (s)he has had with you
The nature of those outside interactions (example: research advisor)

In paragraph 2 (and possibly 3): the author should briefly state his/her overall impression of you as a student. Then, (s)he should mention the specific qualities that you demonstrated in his/her classroom. Bear in mind, whether you are writing a letter or requesting one for yourself, the power is in the details. Do not simply mention the grade the candidate earned in the class. Instead, take the time to document the specific talents or skills the person demonstrated to earn that grade.

For example, in science and math classes, students must use their analytical and quantitative skills to solve practical problems. Professors in these classes should document the candidate's critical thinking skills; if the professor supervised a laboratory class, (s)he should also document the candidate's mastery of scientific principles and various analytical methods.

Likewise, students who major in journalism, English, education, and business are expected to be excellent communicators. Professors from these disciplines should provide an objective assessment of the candidate's ability to speak and write in a clear, logical, and persuasive manner.

Finally, artistic students, such as writers, painters, and musicians, are usually creative and independent thinkers who have the confidence to express themselves through their work. Professors should document their talent, motivation, and skill.

Regardless of the candidate's background, the author should focus on *one or two exceptional traits* that (s)he has personally observed that person demonstrate in the classroom. The letter should document those strengths and offer a specific example to support the praise.

For example, if a letter claims that a candidate is a good writer, the author must mention a specific paper or assignment that the candidate completed in an extraordinary way. What was the topic? The length? What was terrific about the paper – was it short, concise, well documented, or unusually insightful? Be specific.

In the next paragraph: All students, regardless of their background or major, are expected to demonstrate a strong love of learning and the appropriate level of respect for their fellow students. Authors should document these points in the following paragraph, by mentioning the candidate's participation in class, willingness to help others, and attendance at office hours. If appropriate, the author should also document the candidate's ability to work in a team environment. Is (s)he a natural leader? Did (s)he pull his/her weight on any class projects or presentations? If so, offer specific details.

In the penultimate paragraph: mention any other notable facts about the candidate that you want to convey. This section of the letter has the most flexibility, depending upon the candidate's background and what you have personally observed. Good points to include:

a. Participation in outside activities related the candidate's major (or a legal career)
b. Practical experience in the candidate's major, through internships, summer work, or paid employment
c. The ability to succeed in the face of adversity. As we discussed in Chapter 5, this can be tricky if the candidate does not want you to reveal the information. Nevertheless, there are situations in which the committee cannot properly assess the candidate's character and motivation unless they know the whole story.

From our perspective, the following factors are worth mentioning:

a. The candidate earned excellent grades while working full-time to support himself/herself.
b. The candidate graduated on time, despite suffering a life-threatening illness or injury.
c. The candidate has documented learning disabilities, but did not request special accommodations in the classroom (or for the LSAT).
d. The candidate was a top performer, despite wrestling with serious personal challenges at home (divorce, death, familial illness, language or cultural barriers).

Although these issues are private – and deeply difficult to talk about – the way a candidate deals with them is an indication of his/her maturity and character. If you have the applicant's permission to mention the issue – and you are willing to do so – you can provide the committee with insight into the candidate's life that they could not acquire any other way.

In the final paragraph: put your opinion of the candidate into the proper perspective. How many students have you taught in your entire career? How does the candidate compare to that group – the top 1%, 5%, or 20%? If you have specific experience with students who have obtained a law degree, it is particularly helpful to compare the candidate to that group. If the applicant is equally intelligent, motivated, and dynamic, this is the place to mention it.

In the closing statement: offer a brief summary of the candidate's qualifications and state the strength of your recommendation (enthusiastic, without reservation, etc.). In the last sentence, you should provide your contact information (phone number and email address) in case the committee wants to confirm your letter or acquire additional details. Although it is highly unlikely that someone will contact you, your letter will have an added level of credibility if you indicate that you are receptive to further contact.

Finally, print your letter on your official letterhead and sign it as follows:

John Smith, Ph.D.   (Name, Academic Degree)
Professor of English   (Formal Title)
Harvard University   (Affiliation)

Here are several recommendation letters for law school candidates that were written by seasoned faculty members. To protect the privacy of the writer and applicant, the names of all people, classes, schools, places, and companies have been changed.

Letter #1: From Professor

Please accept this letter of support for Eric Ryan's application for law school. Eric is currently a senior at the University of Minnesota, where I am an Associate Professor of Psychology. I have known Eric since he first visited our campus during his senior year of high school. In his four years with us, he has completed four of my classes and has been one of our most successful undergraduate students. From my observation, Eric has strong potential for success in any discipline he chooses.

In addition to his considerable academic strengths, Eric is a gifted and prolific researcher. As a junior, he enrolled in Psycho-Biological Research Methodology, a graduate-level course which required students to complete an entire research project (from literature review to final paper) in just one semester. Eric tackled his project with gusto and completed his paper in time to present his results at the annual American Psychological Research Symposium (APRS) in Augusta, Georgia. Without a doubt, Eric's presentation was one of the best at the conference. He demonstrated remarkable composure, particularly during the grueling question-and-answer session, in which he was besieged with inquiries that went beyond the scope of his work. I was impressed by Eric's ability to think on his feet under such stressful circumstances.

During his senior year, Eric completed a follow-up project to address the questions he had been asked at the previous APRS conference. His subsequent presentation at the annual meeting won first place in the undergraduate research competition. To my delight, Eric has already begun to build a professional network at these conferences by chatting with peers from other institutions about their research. His intellectual curiosity is unparalleled for someone his age.

In his latest project, Eric developed a novel questionnaire for use in surveys with grade school participants. Unlike traditional forms, which require a fourth-grade literacy level, Eric's form uses a clever combination of symbols and scales to solicit data from younger subjects. Upon its presentation at the 2008 APRS, the questionnaire caught the eye of Dr. Glenn Rayburn, the President and CEO of Omega Marketing, Inc. Seeing its potential for use in evaluating children's products, Eric patented the form and is currently negotiating a licensing agreement with Dr. Rayburn's firm. As you might expect, Eric's success in developing and marketing a product for consumer use has been an exciting and inspirational experience for our entire department. We are quite proud of what he has been able to achieve in such a short period of time.

Eric has completed four of my classes, including Social & Developmental Psychology and the Psychology of Addictions. He is an exceptional student: intelligent, enthusiastic and assertive. Eric's insightful comments, peppered with his wry sense of humor, invariably brought our classroom discussions to a higher level. From my observation, Eric's writing and reasoning skills are comparable to those of the doctoral candidates in our department. He has a bright future in academic research, if he chooses to pursue it.

As his advisor, I have been most impressed by Eric's strong sense of moral responsibility. When the University of Minnesota implemented an Honor Code in 2009, Eric was one of its strongest supporters. In class, Eric eloquently explained how the Honor Code would enhance the reputation of all Minnesota graduates, because it would assure future employers that a candidate's grades were earned honestly. I respected Eric's willingness to follow his heart and support an unpopular position. I am certain that he will bring the same strong sense of honor and integrity to law school.

Eric's success is attributable to his rare combination of intelligence, motivation, communication skills and personal strengths. He is an extremely well-balanced young man with the ability to form strong positive relationships with his peers and faculty members. In his leisure time, Eric serves as a volunteer in the campus recruiting office and is involved in a number of community fund-raising projects. As expected, he brings a strong sense of enthusiasm and goodwill to all of these endeavors.

I recommend Eric without hesitation, as he is an outstanding young man in every sense of the word. You will enjoy having him as a student.

<u>Our Assessment</u>: This letter provides an extensive, well-documented discussion of Eric's strengths as a student, researcher and campus leader. In several places, the author explains how the candidate's skills will be useful in law school. From an admissions perspective, the most compelling section of the letter is the paragraph about integrity; Eric's ability and willingness to stand up for his principles impressed every member of the admissions committee. By taking the time to document these exemplary personal strengths, which the committee would not otherwise have known about, this professor gave Eric's candidacy a tangible boost.

Letter #2: From Finance Professor

I am pleased to write this recommendation on behalf of Melinda Bryant, who was a student in the finance program at the University of Pennsylvania between 2004 and 2008. I taught her in two classes and also served as Department Head for the duration of her undergraduate program. During that time, I watched Melinda mature into a poised and accomplished young woman with excellent work habits and superior interpersonal skills. She remains one of my favorite students.

From her first days in my Options & Derivatives class, Melinda demonstrated incomparable diligence, analytical skills and an ability to think on her feet. The class tends to be particularly challenging because a major portion of the grade is based on class presentations. Every week, students were asked to research a series of investment products (stocks, bonds, options, mutual funds, etc.) and to select the one most likely to achieve a specific financial goal. On any given day, students were randomly selected to defend their choices in class. Melinda was an excellent researcher who understood how to apply basic information to specific scenarios. More impressively, she handled difficult (sometimes hostile) questions from her fellow students with grace and confidence. Even when her choice deviated from the "correct" answer, Melinda demonstrated excellent reasoning skills in selecting and defending her choice. She consistently maintained her poise and sense of humor while other students were reduced to tears.

For her senior project in finance, Melinda developed and managed an investment club at a local retirement community. Melinda's job was to recruit the participants and explain the risk/reward profile of various investment options. Throughout the semester, Melinda did an exceptional job explaining the different stock sectors to 36 novice investors. She patiently answered questions, discussed brokerage house options, and taught the participants how to research their picks on the Internet. The group not only made money; they had great fun. Throughout the semester, I watched Melinda become more confident in her ability to manage a challenging project. The investment club was an unqualified success, largely because of her dedication.

In addition to her academic success in our rigorous finance program, Melinda is also a talented vocalist with strong ties to community theatre. In late 2007, while performing in "The Marriage of Figaro," Melinda became fascinated by the short story upon which the opera was based. We enjoyed several after-class discussions about the work, whose meaning is often debated by seasoned literary critics. Melinda became intrigued by the work's subtleties, noting that its interpretation depended upon the language in which it was read; the French to English translation of specific words created considerable ambiguity. After reading the French version of the story, Melinda wrote a superb analysis of the compromises inherent in the English translation. Her essay was flawless, including a logical and insightful analysis. The paper remains a crown jewel in the English literature department.

Melinda is a motivated young woman of numerous talents and considerable self-discipline. Whether studying derivative curves, writing an essay, or preparing for an operatic performance, she gives each endeavor her full focus and attention. This passion and determination are rare and precious gifts.

In over twenty-five years of teaching, I have known few other students with Melinda's talent and drive. I am certain that she will be an asset to both student life and academic excellence at XXXXXXX Law School.

<u>Our Assessment</u>: This letter was written by a well-known professor at the University of Pennsylvania. Its strength is that the author clearly knows the applicant well and is favorably impressed by her work. The writer did a great job of citing specific examples of Melinda's financial expertise and community service work. She also documented the candidate's unusual skills as a vocalist and writer. By citing Melinda's tenacity and discipline, she distinguished her from the hundreds of other applicants with similar academic achievements.

Letter #3: From Literary Professor

I am pleased to recommend Olivia Barns for admission to your institution. I have known Olivia for three years as a student in my creative writing classes. During that time, she proved to be a creative, industrious and prolific writer.

In the classroom, Olivia was a joy to work with. She constantly strove to produce innovative manuscripts about the real-life challenges of women. In my Creative Fiction III class, I encouraged Olivia to submit her work to the mainstream press. By the end of the semester, Olivia had four short stories accepted for publication in national magazines. Her future in creative writing is whatever she chooses to make it.

Olivia demonstrated her impressive skills as a researcher while completing her senior class paper, "Women in British Literature." As part of her research, Olivia took the initiative to locate and interview several direct descendants of Jane Austen, who provided invaluable insight into the author's motivation and perspective. Elizabeth Reed, the great-grandniece of Ms. Austen, graciously provided Olivia with Jane's original notes for "Pride and Prejudice," which had never been made available to the public. Olivia's paper included a rich discussion of Ms. Austen's private thoughts on several notable historical events, which are eloquently captured in her writing. After reading Olivia's paper, I had a greater understanding of life in Ms. Austen's time and the challenges she faced as an author. I subsequently re-read "Pride and Prejudice" with a more enlightened perspective. Thanks to Olivia's herculean efforts, her paper was a magnificent example of narrative and descriptive writing.

Outside the classroom, Olivia has lent her writing and editing skills to several volunteer organizations, including the Denver chapter of Planned Parenthood. In 2007, Olivia authored a twelve-page brochure that described their available services. She also scripted their commercials for local television. As expected, her material was well written, well organized and well received in the community. I admire her willingness to lend her skills to a group that she is passionate about.

By actively seeking opportunities to write, including freelance assignments for national magazines, Olivia already earns her living as a published author. She is an inspiration to other students and faculty members who "can't find the time" to pursue their own projects. On several occasions, Olivia has graciously offered to help her fellow students with their manuscripts. In our 2008 summer creative writing conference, she demonstrated excellent project management skills in compiling a collection of students' short stories about September 11. As expected, several were accepted for publication in national magazines.

Overall, Olivia is a talented, conscientious and dedicated woman. I am certain that she has the abilities and drive to accomplish almost anything she sets her mind to. She will inevitably become an attorney of incomparable eloquence and skill.

Our Assessment: This letter provides a short and well-documented discussion of Olivia's achievements as a writer. She is clearly a woman who is willing to use her skills on behalf of interests and causes that are significant to her. The committee was impressed not only by Olivia's many publications, but by her kind heart and charitable nature. Her interest in public interest law was a great fit for the law school that she eventually chose.

Letter #4: From Law Professor

My name is William DeFrantorio. For the past ten years, I have taught business law classes at Temple University. I am also a criminal defense attorney with twenty-six years of legal experience. I have been asked by Frank Hansen to write a letter of recommendation in his bid to pursue a law degree. I am pleased that Frank has decided to focus his energy in a direction that clearly befits his character.

During the past four years, Frank has been a student in three of my classes in civil and criminal law. I was impressed by his ability to glean the unseen truths and obstacles in the case studies we discussed. Frank exhibited a strong interest in the subjects of negligence, strict liability and market share liability, taking particular interest in the high profile cases involving the manufacturers of Tylenol, silicone breast implants, and Jif peanut butter. A stickler for details, Frank sometimes became irritated when a fact was misinterpreted during a class discussion. In all assignments, Frank had obviously done his homework.

After the Supreme Court's examination of racial discrimination/affirmative action in law school admission at the University of Michigan (Gratz/Grutter/Hammacher v. Bollinger), Frank produced a thorough and well-written analysis of the decision, arguing at length in support of Justice Smith's controversial ruling. Although some of the students resisted class debates because of stage fright, Frank aggressively engaged in the forum and showed an ongoing desire for intellectual challenge.

Frank's skills as a speaker were particularly well-utilized during his presidency of the Law Club, in which he participated in several mock trials. As the faculty advisor for the group, I witnessed the dedication and enthusiasm that Frank brought to preparing and presenting a case. He excelled at all aspects of the process, from initial research through delivery of his final argument. I could see how energized he was by the process, carefully noting the "juror" reaction to even subtle points of law. Even when he was on the losing side, Frank refused to surrender without a fight. He clearly has it in him to become a great trial attorney.

At my urging, Frank spent the past two summers as a law clerk for the City of Philadelphia. He reported directly to Mayor John Jones, who nurtured Frank's interests in community affairs. Frank worked closely with Mayor Jones to draft legislation to prevent further development of Philadelphia's unincorporated areas. Frank and I enjoyed several fruitful discussions about what he learned about the environmental hazards of over-development. His experience in public interest law has made him more cognizant of the underlying conflict of interest between developers and environmentalists.

After several decades in academia, I believe that I am a good judge of character. In the years I have known Frank, I can vouch for his enthusiastic interest in the law and his dogged pursuit of the truth. After our first exam, Frank spent considerable time with me working through the problems that he had answered wrong. He is academically gifted and thirsty for a challenge. I suspect that my classes in business and criminal law have confirmed his decision to attend law school. If so, I am proud to have been a catalyst in this exceptional student's career path. The law school that admits Frank Hansen will be greatly enhanced by his presence.

<u>Our Assessment</u>: This author, a noted defense attorney, rarely offers such effusive praise on behalf of a candidate. Accordingly, his detailed discussion of Frank's strengths as a student and law clerk made a positive impression on the committee.

Letter #5: Documents Moot Court Participation

It is with great honor that I recommend Ms. Ingrid Zamora to your institution. She is one of the best students I have taught in my twenty-year career at Princeton.

I first met Ms. Zamora in 2007, when I served as the Professor in her class in International Economics. From the start, she demonstrated a strong native intelligence and a superior work ethic, which enabled her to analyze ambiguous – and often conflicting – data from multiple perspectives. Whenever I posed a question, I could count on Ms. Zamora to offer an insightful opinion and respond to the points raised by other students. In speech and in writing, she identified the core issues and offered a clear and well-reasoned response, without being distracted by extraneous factors. Based on her excellent performance on three written exams and an oral presentation, I awarded Ms. Zamora 98 points (out of 100) in the course.

A year later, I served as the advisor for Ms. Zamora's team during the 2008 International Collegiate Moot Court Competition in Washington, D.C. As the team leader, Ms. Zamora assumed the responsibility for consolidating and finalizing her team members' individual arguments, which required a massive amount of work. To do so, Ms. Zamora conducted original research on a case that involved an unprecedented intellectual property issue in China, which carried a huge burden of proof and had never been resolved by an international court. To complicate our challenge, we soon realized that the advisor for the competitive team was a distinguished expert on the matter, who would bring an unfair advantage to the proceedings.

Despite these obstacles, Ms. Zamora did not let us down. By harnessing the diverse strengths of her teammates, she developed a logical and cohesive argument that incorporated evidence from five different appellate courts. Ms. Zamora also revealed an impressive ability to perform in a crisis. The night before her presentation, she learned that one of her team members had been called away from the proceedings due to a family emergency. With little advance warning, Ms. Zamora agreed to handle both presentations, which required meticulous preparation.

To my delight, her performance was nothing short of extraordinary. Ms. Zamora delivered two impassioned arguments and eloquently fielded questions from the judges. Her remarkable performance earned her rare praise from Judge Laughton Mlies, who aptly noted that she was a "natural litigator." At the end of the competition, Ms. Zamora received the award for Best Overall Performance in the event, which included a $25,000 scholarship prize. Thanks to her extraordinary skills as a speaker, writer, and organizer, our team also tied for First Prize in this distinguished competition.

Upon our return to campus, I offered Ms. Zamora a position as a research assistant in my department. It was the first - and only – time I have extended such an offer to an undergraduate student. In subsequent months, my trust in her has proven to be well placed. Ms. Zamora has conducted basic research for me on two economic studies about Haiti, which required her to read, analyze, and compile information from several divergent sources. The amount of work she has completed – and the quality of her analyses – is nothing short of extraordinary.

Compared to her peers, Ms. Zamora will bring a rare level of intelligence and passion to your program. She is also a natural leader who sets a positive example for others. Looking ahead, I am certain that Ms. Zamora will succeed in whatever capacity she chooses – politics, public service, or private practice. I offer her my strongest possible endorsement.

<u>Our Assessment</u>: Before they read this letter, the admissions committee had not received third party confirmation of this candidate's skills as an orator. The author, who was a distinguished professor at Princeton, took the time to document her performance at a highly stressful international competition. By supporting the material in her personal statement in such an enthusiastic way, the writer gave her application the boost that it needed in a competitive applicant pool.

Chapter 7:   Letters from Employers / Supervisors

In addition to a letter from a faculty member, law schools will also accept a letter from a candidate's employer (or supervisor).   For older candidates who are working full-time, this letter should document your professional achievements since you graduated from college, which can give you an edge over more recent graduates.   Ideally, the letter should be written by your direct supervisor (or another person in your chain of command).

If you cannot provide a letter from your boss without jeopardizing your job, you should submit a letter from a client or peer, rather than a supervisor.   But you MUST send a letter from someone who can document your performance in your most recent position.   As we discussed in Chapter 2, the "ideal" person to write your letter is someone who:

a.   understands the intellectual demands of law school
b.   knows you well enough to evaluate your qualifications
c.   is willing/able to provide enough supporting detail to justify his/her assessment

Letters from supervisors should include the following information:

a.   the type and extent of your professional experiences
b.   your career progression thus far, including any awards or promotions
c.   the specific skills you use in your position (and how they relate to a legal career)
d.   your personality and stamina.

In Paragraph 1, the author should explain his/her relationship with you, including:

His/her title and employer
How long (s)he has known you
Your relationship to him/her
The nature (and extent) of your professional interactions

In paragraph 2 (and possibly 3):   the author should briefly state his/her overall impression of you as a candidate.   Then, (s)he should mention the specific qualities that you have demonstrated in your interactions with him/her.   Remember, for law school recommendation letters, the power is in the details.   Do not simply list the candidate's job duties. Instead, take the time to document the *specific talents or skills* the person has demonstrated in that position.

Obviously, a candidate's accomplishments will depend upon his/her education and job title.   No two applicants will be exactly alike, which means that there is no "right" or "wrong" information for an author to include.   Our best advice is to describe the person's accountabilities - and how well (s)he has fulfilled them.   But don't simply offer a laundry list of responsibilities; instead, you should focus on *one or two exceptional traits* that you have personally observed the candidate demonstrate in your interactions with him/her.

Ideally, the letter will also include specific examples to support the praise.   For example, if a letter claims that a candidate is a good writer, the author must mention a specific paper or assignment that the candidate completed in an extraordinary way.   What was the topic? The length?   What was terrific about the paper – was it short, concise, well documented, or unusually insightful?   Be specific.

In the next paragraph: All candidates, regardless of their background or profession, are expected to demonstrate the general character traits that law schools value, which are listed on the rating scale.   They include:

1.   Intellectual curiosity, common sense
2.   Motivation, reliability, perseverance
3.   Judgment, resourcefulness, communication skills
4.   Interpersonal skills, emotional stability, self-confidence, empathy, maturity

Authors should document these points in the following paragraph, by mentioning the candidate's habits and relationships at work.   Is (s)he motivated, resourceful, and reliable?   Does (s)he require a lot of direction or very little?   Does (s)he coast by or constantly look for new ways to contribute?   Document it in the letter.   If possible, the author should also document the candidate's ability to work in a team environment.   Is (s)he a natural leader?   Did (s)he pull his/her weight on any team projects or presentations?   If so, offer specific details.

In the penultimate paragraph: mention any other notable facts about the candidate that you want to convey. This section of the letter has the most flexibility, depending upon the candidate's background and what you have personally observed. Good points to include:

a. Participation in outside activities that relate to the candidate's job (or a legal career)
b. The ability to succeed in the face of adversity. As we discussed in Chapter 5, this can be tricky if the candidate does not want you to reveal the information. Nevertheless, there are situations in which the committee cannot properly assess the candidate's character and motivation unless they know the whole story.

From our perspective, the following factors are worth mentioning:

a. The candidate was a top performer, despite wrestling with serious personal challenges at home (divorce, death, familial illness, language or cultural barriers).
b. The candidate faced a daunting challenge in his/her job, but handled it in a mature and inspirational way.

Although these issues are private – and deeply difficult to talk about – the way a candidate deals with them is an indication of his/her maturity and character. If you have the applicant's permission to mention the issue – and you are willing to do so – you can provide the committee with insight into the candidate's life that they never could have acquired any other way.

In the final paragraph: put your opinion of the candidate into the proper perspective How many people have you supervised at the candidate's level? How does the candidate compare to that group – the top 1%, 5%, or 20%? If you have specific experience with candidates who have obtained a law degree, it is particularly helpful to compare the candidate to that group. If the applicant is equally intelligent, motivated, and dynamic, this is the place to mention it.

In the closing statement: offer a brief summary of the candidate's qualifications and state the strength of your recommendation (enthusiastic, without reservation, etc.). In the last sentence, you should provide your contact information (phone number and email address) in case the committee wants to confirm your letter or acquire additional details. Although it is highly unlikely that someone will contact you, your letter will have an added level of credibility if you make yourself accessible to the reader.

Finally, print your letter on your official letterhead and sign it as follows:

John Smith, J.D.　　　　　Name, Academic Degree
Attorney　　　　　　　　　Formal Title
Smith & Wesson Law Firm　Affiliation

Here are several recommendation letters for law school candidates that were written by their supervisors. To protect the privacy of the writer and applicant, the names of all people, classes, schools, places, and companies have been changed.

Letter #6: From Supervisor

I am happy to recommend Adam Wexler for admission to law school. Adam worked under my direct supervision as a Graphic Artist and Designer for a five-year period at Precise Advertising, which handles the marketing and advertising needs for several international consumer product companies. Overall, he was an excellent employee who fulfilled the duties of his position in an exemplary way.

As an artist and designer, Adam consistently produced high quality work in a timely fashion. When asked, he always came up with ideas for our clients that were innovative and fresh. Adam's first project was the advertising campaign for Starkist Tuna, which was a $12 million dollar account. By the time the Starkist team approached us, they had already screened and rejected most of our competitors. Landing their business was a long shot, but we accomplished it, thanks mostly to Adam. After researching their target market, he came up with a creative concept for their television and print ads that touted the health benefits of tuna for women and children. This resonated strongly with the Starkist CEO, who was looking for a way to capture the juvenile market. At their insistence, Adam became the point person for the account and handled all of their creative issues. The feedback we received about Adam was overwhelmingly positive.

Adam also produced great work on the technical side of the business. On his own initiative, Adam completed a web design class and quickly became our in-house expert at Dreamweaver and Flash animation. Whenever possible, he used the technology in our ad campaigns and on our newly redesigned website. Adam's most recent technical achievement was adding a digitized video stream to the web site, which allows us to showcase our most promising ad concepts to prospective clients without incurring the travel costs of traditional sales calls. In the ten months it has been on the site, the video stream has attracted nearly 300,000 hits and has generated dozens of inquiries for our services. In late 2007, we were named the Most Creative Site by the American Advertising Council, out of more than 200 sites on the internet. We couldn't be more pleased by this positive response.

During his tenure with us, Adam matured into an excellent manager. When he assumed responsibility for the Starkist account, he became a supervisor for the first time, which required him to coordinate the work of two junior artists and a technician. At first, Adam seemed overwhelmed by the responsibility and was tempted to micromanage his people. Fortunately, early on, he took the initiative to have several constructive discussions with his team members about expectations and communication. They quickly learned to work together; afterwards, they delivered all projects within their time and budget restrictions.

Adam recently left the firm when his wife accepted a faculty position at the University of California at Los Angeles. We discussed his interest in obtaining a law degree at the time of his departure. Knowing Adam as well as I do, I think it is an excellent career choice for him. He is a hard working man, analytical by nature, who communicates well with others. He is loyal to a fault and not afraid to champion a worthy cause or to resolve a professional disagreement. In all situations, he handles himself with grace and good humor. You will enjoy having him as a student.

I have no hesitation in recommending Adam Wexler for your program. Should you require further elaboration, don't hesitate to contact me at 555-555-5555.

<u>Our Assessment</u>: This letter not only sells the candidate's technical and administrative strengths, but puts a positive spin on his early difficulties as a manager. By citing Adam's ability to negotiate with his team and build a productive relationship with them, the author highlights his maturity and judgment. His comments were well-perceived.

Letter #7: From Manager: Documents the Candidate's Strong Administrative Skills

I have worked with Frank Ford for over five years at Adelphi Software, where I am the President and CEO. After serving as our creative manager during the company's startup, Frank rapidly assumed responsibility for all aspects of systems administration. Thanks to his diligence and creativity, we have enjoyed continual expansion and revenue growth ($1.7 million to $28 million in just five years).

When Frank first approached me about the job, he said he was willing to do "whatever it took" to prove his worth. Since then, he has far exceeded my expectations, both through the volume of his work and the conscientiousness he has brought to the firm. Under Frank's direction, Adelphi Software has survived the rapid consolidation and outsourcing in the technology industry. Frank created his department from the ground up, setting the standards for our software and handling all aspects of troubleshooting and quality control. Frank is responsible for all technical aspects of the business, including our computer network and databases. He also works "in the trenches" with our manufacturing team in China to set an example of efficiency and productivity.

Frank's responsibilities require a rare combination of technical, administrative and interpersonal strengths. Fortunately, he handles all of these challenges with confidence. Frank is a quintessential "team player;" in leadership situations, he is the glue that holds the team together, creating a healthy environment for a creative exchange of ideas. Whenever possible, he offers guidance and training to subordinates who want to learn more. By employing these strengths, Frank's work teams are highly successful and often surpass our clients' expectations.

Frank's greatest accomplishment is the database that he created to streamline and centralize communication and production within the company. Frank rallied for the change throughout his first two years with the firm and ultimately took the initiative to develop the system himself. I was amazed by its effectiveness and ease of use. Frank's custom database solution eliminates the paperwork and communication issues that plague most software firms. It has literally revolutionized the way we do business. What was most impressive was Frank's initiative and motivation. He completed the project on his own time, with no prodding from senior management and no guarantee of success. His goal was not self-promotion, but to improve the way the company functions.

Analytical by nature, Frank is a fast learner with an impressive command of software technology. He troubleshoots complicated situations with ease, simultaneously computing multiple scenarios to identify the optimal solution. To a lay person, it seems like Frank simply "knows" the answer, when he is actually applying years of training and skill to each situation. Even under stressful circumstances, he has an amazing ability to remember and apply standards and technical rules.

Thankfully, Frank is also able to communicate with others, including those with non-technical backgrounds. Frank routinely prepares and delivers project presentations to clients and senior managers. He has an excellent command of English and a polished presentation style. On a personal level, Frank has a congenial personality and a great sense of humor. He is honest to a fault and highly supportive of those around him.

Frank's chief drawback is his tendency to be a perfectionist and expect too much from himself. During his first years with the firm, he resisted delegating because he was afraid that his employees would not complete the tasks correctly. Fortunately, Frank has learned to better pace himself and manage his time. By doing so, he has increased the quality and quantity of work that he can deliver. Not surprisingly, he has also become a more nurturing manager who allows his people to shine

Throughout my career, I have retained several talented attorneys to handle the legal aspects of my business. I am certain that Frank Ford possesses the requisite talent to handle similar responsibilities. If you would like additional details about Frank, please feel free to contact me at 555-555-5555.

<u>Our Assessment</u>: This letter provides an excellent personal and professional endorsement for a seasoned technical manager. Although the author could not state *why* the candidate wanted to go to law school, he convinced the reader that Frank was certainly up to the task. Fortunately, one of Frank's other recommendations explained his long-term goals, including his longstanding interest in working for a non-profit group. As a result, the committee was better able to understand Frank's motivation for making a career change at this point in time.

Letter #8: From Employer / Supervisor

I have known Diana Caldwell since 1997, when she joined the advertising department of *Runner's Daily* magazine. In 2005, Diana moved to our Boston office on a special assignment to establish our company's Internet presence. When Diana returned to head office in 2008, she became my employee, since I had been promoted to Vice President of Advertising Operations the previous year.

From her first days at the magazine, Diana demonstrated an amazing flair for sales and advertising. At the time, *Runner's Daily* had never tried to permeate the markets outside Canada and the United States. Diana's charge was to sell advertising for an eclectic group of corporate clients in Europe, Asia and South America who were unfamiliar with our publication. Despite her young age, Diana performed her primary role in an efficient and professional manner. Utilizing her command of French, Spanish and German, she forged several successful relationships with our European advertisers and distributors, who helped her to make additional business contacts. In just three years, *Runner's Daily* achieved a 40% market share in Europe, which exceeded our highest expectations. Even in Asia, where women rarely conducted business transactions, Diana made significant inroads with key advertisers.

Diana also excelled at the analytical aspects of the job, which required her to gather and analyze data from diverse parties and make complex financial projections. Diana's analyses were subsequently used to select the lowest cost vendors. In this capacity, she demonstrated that she was a quick learner and an excellent multi-tasker. I was particularly impressed by how quickly and seamlessly Diana was able to provide support to the Accounting Group during our annual audits, which required her to learn how to process complex financial transactions.

After five years as an advertising assistant, Diana was promoted to copywriter in 2002, a position that she held for nearly three years. As an advertising copywriter and direct marketing expert, she is among the best in the business. Diana has a gift for writing, and her creative mind was responsible for some of the most successful marketing campaigns that *Runner's Daily* has ever implemented. In 2004, Diana was hand-picked by senior management to work in Atlanta with the Internet Project Team. As team leader, she led the group responsible for adapting our direct mail campaigns to the Internet. The company implemented the team's strategy in early 2006, making *Runner's Daily* one of the top three publishing companies on the Web.

During the 2008 recession, our company endured a major downsizing event, which reduced our total headcount from 1200 to 180. Diana was one of the few people to survive the layoffs, because she was simply too valuable to let go. When her group disbanded, Diana stayed on as a manager in our training department. With her strong background in languages, Diana was uniquely qualified to train new employees to implement the company's mailing campaigns across the globe. She has been highly successful in this capacity, increasing our subscription revenues in Asia by 69% in just one fiscal year. Thanks to Diana, *Runner's Daily* has established a solid presence in Asian markets that were formerly considered impenetrable.

On an interpersonal basis, Diana is truly a pleasure to work with. She displays a friendly, helpful and outgoing demeanor at all times. Consequently, she is well-liked by both her colleagues and managers. In hindsight, I am certain that Diana's pleasant demeanor with our multicultural clientele has generated significant revenue for us. She has an intuitive understanding of the service aspect of our business.

In closing, as I hope the above clearly attests, I think that Diana Caldwell is an exceptionally bright and hardworking individual who throws herself enthusiastically into whatever she undertakes. Accordingly, I have no hesitation whatsoever in recommending Diana for admission to law school.

<u>Our Assessment</u>: The strength of this letter is that it documents Diana's impressive track record of career advancement in a declining industry. It also provides specific examples of strengths that are highly prized in the admissions process. Even small details, such as Diana's background in foreign languages, enhanced the committee's positive opinion of her.

Letter #9:   From Supervisor

I am delighted to write a reference letter to support Clive Bradley's application to law school.   I have worked with Clive for nearly four years at Xenon Corporation, where I am the Director of Technology in the Software Division. Throughout this time, Clive has enjoyed a series of promotions from Design Engineer to Project Manager in the Information Technology department.   Due to Xenon's unusual organizational structure, Clive has been my direct report in all of these assignments.

In his current position, Clive supervises software development teams in sites throughout North America. He also leads the consulting team that provides software solutions to semi-conductor companies in Europe and South America.   In this capacity, Clive is responsible for the entire project management cycle, from the initial concept through the final execution.   On a daily basis, Clive is responsible for resource allocation, manpower coordination as well as answering questions from team members and customers.   He also resolves all technical issues and coordinates the timing of their work.

Clive is an excellent project manager with a clear focus on the bottom-line.   In his first year with the company, he proposed and implemented the "paperless project," which converted all of our paper files into electronic media.   To reduce costs and improve efficiency, Clive also proposed and designed a web solution that is now used as a template across all departments.   Despite the firm's initial resistance to the idea, Clive documented its benefits and convinced senior managers to give it a try.   Ultimately, Clive's suggestion to use customized templates eliminated the need to develop applications from scratch, which saved considerable time and money.

Clive is a fast learner with an impressive command of software technology.   When one of his colleagues left the firm without notice, Clive took over the project from scratch and supported it within one week.   He constantly seeks out new challenges and opportunities for growth.   When one of his colleagues feared that she wasn't up to speed on all departmental projects, Clive proposed a weekly technology luncheon, at which team members would take turns discussing their top projects. In addition to their brainstorming effects, the luncheons have made the group more cohesive.   They have also helped the team members improve their presentation skills.   Clive, in particular, has become a polished speaker who gives lively and engaging technical presentations.

Clive's only drawback is his tendency to try to take on too many projects at once.   In some ways, this is an embarrassment of riches, because most of his ideas are viable ways to increase business and reduce costs.   As his supervisor, I have helped Clive manage this tendency by setting clearly defined goals and priorities on projects of corporate-level interest.   Clive has subsequently gained positive attention from senior management and has earned a reputation as a "fast tracker" within the department.

With legal training, Clive will be in an excellent position to work in intellectual property law, particularly as it relates to computer technology.   In ten years, I can easily envision Clive serving as legal counsel to a major software company, either as an employee or in an advisory capacity.   With his combined strengths in languages, technology and the law, he will be well-positioned to be a leader in his field.

I am delighted by Clive's decision to enter law school.   If you would like additional information about Clive, please feel free to contact me at 555-555-5555 or at email@host.com.

<u>Our Assessment</u>:   This author highlights not only Clive's technical skills, but his strengths as a manager.   He also provides an honest assessment of Clive's weakness and how he helped him to overcome it.   By providing a balanced perspective of Clive's performance, the author came across as more honest and credible.   He also did an excellent job of citing Clive's particular fit for intellectual property law.

Letter #10:   From Supervisor (Sales)

I am pleased to write a letter of recommendation on behalf of Samantha Brown, who has worked as the National Sales Director for Holmes Medical Supply for the past six years.   In this role, she has created and maintained our sales in the lower 48 states and represented our firm at several North American trade shows. She has also supervised the work of eight Regional Sales Managers, who are located in different cities.   By supervising Samantha during this period, I have gained a realistic assessment of the many skills she will bring to the legal profession.

When Samantha came onboard, Holmes had eight regional sales offices with no national manager – as a result, they tended to work independently.   Samantha faced several challenges to coordinate the work of her sales people, who were scattered in different locations across the United States.   Thankfully, she is a highly organized woman with extraordinary analytical skills.   During her first weeks on the job, Samantha reviewed our records to identify ways we could gain additional business from our existing accounts.   She also assessed the needs and trends in the industry –from a technical, manufacturing, and business standpoint – to solve problems and identify new sales opportunities.

Samantha exhibited superior skills in this area, which is critical in our business.   She identified many new sales leads in unexplored areas, such as military and veteran's hospitals, which were highly profitable for Holmes.   Samantha's dynamic personality was a considerable asset to her in this process - she was gracious enough to work effectively with an eclectic group of people to negotiate the military contracts.   At the same time, she was tenacious enough to gather the voluminous documentation that these government accounts required.

Thanks to Samantha, we enjoyed 65% annual sales growth between 2004 and 2008, mostly due to the lucrative new accounts that she landed.   Her performance, on both a qualitative and quantitative basis, consistently exceeded my expectations.   In my career, I have rarely met anyone as disciplined and motivated as Samantha.   Although she had no prior experience in the medical industry, she quickly brought herself up to speed on our needs and expectations.   She also acquired our certification as an official government vendor, which is extremely difficult to do.   During her six years at Holmes, Samantha has proven to be equally successful at procuring new business and maintaining and growing our existing accounts. Our feedback from customers- including some of the top CEOs in the health care industry- has been exemplary.

On a personal level, Samantha has also grown into a competent and effective manager.   When she first joined our team, Samantha faced a difficult challenge: to supervise people in a field in which she had little or no experience.   From the start, Samantha took the time to establish a solid rapport with her Regional Sales Managers, who had already built successful relationships with our biggest clients.   After earning their trust and support, she quickly got up to speed on our greatest opportunities and challenges.   I attribute Samantha's smooth transition at least partially to the mature and respectful way that she treated her colleagues.

Samantha is also one of the most effective sales people I have ever known.   When she visits a prospective client, she is literally prepared for anything – she has conducted her research, assessed the competition, and developed a winning sales proposition for the client.   Then, when she delivers her pitch, Samantha calmly and methodically eliminates any objection the prospect has about doing business with us.   As a result, Samantha has an impressive record for closing deals in a highly competitive industry.   These skills will undoubtedly serve her well in the legal profession.

Looking ahead, I am certain that Samantha has what it takes to succeed as an attorney.   Throughout her career, she has faced – and conquered - considerable obstacles to success, including the prejudice against women in a male dominated industry.   Most impressively, Samantha has done so with an uncommon level of grace and integrity.   If given the chance, she will be an excellent lawyer.

Please contact me at XXX-XXX-XXXX or at email address if you require additional information.

Our Assessment: This letter, which was written by the CEO of a top medical supply company, verified the candidate's extraordinary sales skills, which were not articulated anywhere else in her application.   The letter also documents her initiative in pursuing military accounts and her ability to close deals that require considerable documentation and flexibility.   Without this letter, the committee might not have seen her as the aggressive self-starter that she is.

Chapter 8:   Letters from Co-Workers, Clients & Peers

In some cases, it is impossible for candidates to provide a letter of recommendation from their current employer without risking their job. The moment their supervisor knows that they are planning to leave their position to go to law school, their future at the firm is in jeopardy. Nevertheless, it is imperative for candidates who are working full-time to provide a letter of recommendation from someone who can document their performance in their current position. Otherwise, it is difficult for the committee to assess the maturity and professional skills the candidate will bring to the table.

If it is impossible to get a reference from someone in your own chain of command, you should submit a letter from a co-worker, client or peer who can provide an objective assessment of your performance. As we discussed in Chapter 2, the "ideal" person to write your letter is someone who:

a.   understands the intellectual demands of law school
b.   knows you well enough to evaluate your qualifications
c.   is willing/able to provide enough supporting detail to justify his/her assessment

Letters from co-workers or peers should include the following information:

a.   the type and extent of your professional experiences
b.   your career progression thus far, including any awards or promotions
c.   the specific skills you use in your position (and how they relate to a legal career)
d.   your personality and stamina

In Paragraph 1, the author should explain his/her relationship with you, including:

His/her title and employer
How long (s)he has known you
Your relationship to him/her
The nature (and extent) of your professional interactions

In paragraph 2 (and possibly 3):, the author should briefly state the *specific talents and skills* the candidate has demonstrated in their professional interactions. Ideally, the letter will also include specific examples to support the praise. For example, if a letter claims that a candidate is a good writer, the author must mention a specific paper or assignment that the candidate completed in an extraordinary way. What was the topic? The length? What was terrific about the paper – was it short, concise, well documented, or unusually insightful? Be specific.

In the next paragraph:. All candidates, regardless of their background or profession, are expected to demonstrate the general character traits that law schools value, which are listed on the rating scale. They include:

1.   Intellectual curiosity, common sense
2.   Motivation, reliability, perseverance
3.   Judgment, resourcefulness, communication skills
4.   Interpersonal skills, emotional stability, self-confidence, empathy, maturity

Authors should document these points by discussing the candidate's habits and relationships at work. Is (s)he motivated, resourceful, and reliable? Does (s)he coast by or constantly look for new ways to contribute? Document it in the letter. If possible, the author should also document the candidate's ability to work in a team environment. Is (s)he a natural leader? Did (s)he pull his/her weight on any team projects or presentations? If so, offer specific details.

In the penultimate paragraph: mention any other notable facts about the candidate that you want to convey.

This section of the letter has the most flexibility, depending upon the candidate's background and what you have personally observed. Good points to include:

a.   Participation in outside activities related the candidate's job (or a legal career)
b.   The ability to succeed in the face of adversity. As we discussed in Chapter 5, this can be tricky if the candidate does not want you to reveal the information. Nevertheless, there are situations in which the committee cannot properly assess the candidate's character and motivation unless they know the whole story.

From our perspective, the following factors are worth mentioning:

a. The candidate was a top performer, despite wrestling with serious personal challenges at home (divorce, death, familial illness, language or cultural barriers).
b. The candidate faced a daunting challenge in his/her job, but handled it in a mature and inspirational way.

Although these issues are private – and deeply difficult to talk about – the way a candidate deals with them is an indication of his/her maturity and character. If you have the applicant's permission to mention the issue – and you are willing to do so – you can provide the committee with insight into the candidate's life that they never could have acquired any other way.

In the final paragraph: put your opinion of the candidate into the proper perspective. How many people have you worked with at the candidate's level? How does the candidate compare to that group – is (s)he in the top 1%, 5%, or 20%? If you have specific experience with candidates who have obtained a law degree, it is particularly helpful to compare the candidate to that group. If the applicant is equally intelligent, motivated, and dynamic, this is the place to mention it.

In the closing statement: offer a brief summary of the person's qualifications and state the strength of your recommendation (enthusiastic, without reservation, etc.). In the last sentence, you should provide your contact information (phone number and email address) in case the committee wants to confirm your letter or acquire additional details. Although it is highly unlikely that someone will contact you, your letter will have an added level of credibility if you make yourself accessible to the reader.

Finally, print your letter on your official letterhead and sign it as follows:

John Smith	Name
Marketing Manager	Formal Title
Kraft, Inc.	Affiliation

Here are several recommendation letters for law school candidates that were written by co-workers, clients and peers. To protect the privacy of the writer and applicant, the names of all people, classes, schools, places, and companies have been changed.

Letter #11:   From a Co-Worker, Client, or Peer

I am honored to write a reference letter for Hazel Gray. I have known Hazel since January of 2006, when she came to work for me at the Pathmark Forensics Laboratory, where I am the Manager of Operations. Over the past three years, Hazel has fulfilled her duties in an excellent manner.

Hazel began as a technician in the front office, where she accepted specimens from our clients for analysis. Then, she completed the formal training program to learn how to perform various serological, microbiological, and histological tests. Although most new employees require a month to complete the training and handle specimens without supervision, Hazel mastered the job within two weeks. Through sheer motivation, Hazel became the fastest and most reliable technician in the front office.

After Hazel graduated from college, we were delighted to hire her on a full-time basis. Because of her success in other departments, we promoted her in October of 2007 to a management position in the laboratory, which handles a variety of physical, chemical and biological analyses. Hazel was promoted to department manager, which required her to restructure one of our busiest and most critical departments. With this promotion, Hazel assumed responsibility for three key functions (sample collection, analysis, and data entry) and twelve employees. Because of the high volume of work and our fast-paced schedule, the previous manager of the laboratory had left in frustration. Hazel stepped into an extremely demanding situation, which forced her to develop her management skills.

As a matter of corporate policy, we guarantee our clients a turnaround time of three to five days for most analytical tests.   At the time of her promotion, Hazel's lab was six weeks behind schedule and unable to catch up. Not surprisingly, Hazel's people were overworked and discouraged. Even more challenging, Hazel found herself in the awkward position of supervising people who had previously been her peers. Fortunately, she had the maturity to handle these circumstances in an amiable manner.

Hazel used a hands-on approach to get her department back on track. She organized teams to eliminate the backlog and to establish an effective schedule for future work. She held departmental meetings to hear everyone's concerns and to improve morale. With no money for raises or promotions, Hazel used creative incentives like candy and snacks to reward her people for a job well done. More importantly, she implemented several procedures to prevent future backlogs and to ensure consistent customer service. Thanks to Hazel's enhanced organizational and interpersonal skills, her department is a model of teamwork and efficiency.

On one occasion, Hazel's computer expertise was a tremendous help to our IT Department. After taking over the department, Hazel questioned whether the data sheet that the front office used could be stored on the computer, rather than written by hand. She worked with the IT department to develop the computerized template that we currently use. The benefits have been tremendous; in addition to saving time in the lab, the new system eliminated one front office position, which freed that employee for other tasks. In a three-month period, the new computerized system stimulated $150,000 in cost savings for Pathmark.

Over the years, Hazel has eagerly accepted every challenge that we presented to her. Because her group handles diverse assignments, Hazel must constantly juggle rigid deadlines and multiple priorities. Fortunately, organization is one of her leading strengths. On any given day, Hazel's group may handle hundreds of specimens from hospitals throughout the city. Even under stressful circumstances, Hazel can be trusted to complete her work flawlessly and graciously. Her ability to manage so many diverse tasks has been an inspiration to many of her colleagues.

Hazel is a bright and hardworking woman who approaches life's challenges with focus and enthusiasm. I am certain that she will bring the same level of determination to your program.

Our Assessment: This is a wonderful letter that captures Hazel's strengths as a manager. For candidates like Hazel, who have spent their entire careers with a single employer, it is critical to obtain a letter that documents the depth and breadth of their professional experience. By the time the reader finishes this letter, (s)he has a better appreciation of what Hazel does and the skills that are required for her to accomplish it.   The author brought Hazel's skills to life in a way that no resume or job description could.

Letter #12: From a Co-Worker, Client, or Peer

Please accept this letter of recommendation for my colleague at Merrill Lynch, Marianne Walters. I have known Marianne since our undergraduate days at Yale, where we were roommates and Tri-Delt sorority sisters. After our graduation in 2002, we both joined Merrill Lynch in Jacksonville as management trainees. We have subsequently worked together on many professional and community projects.

Marianne is by far the most gifted financial analyst at Merrill Lynch. She has an impressive knowledge of finance and an uncanny ability to predict trends in the equity markets. In the eight years we have worked in the Jacksonville office, she has handled the volatile technology sector, including the Internet stocks. For much of 2005 and 2006, Marianne was considered a "contrarian" analyst because she refused to endorse what she felt was an overvalued sector. While many analysts jumped on the technology bandwagon, Marianne wisely held back. Time proved her correct, as the bubble subsequently burst and many "Nasdaq darlings" have failed to recover.

In evaluating a company, Marianne's mantra is always "watch the fundamentals." She has built a successful career by knowing that what's important is not the sizzle of a firm (its advertising or buzz), but the steak (its management strength and P/E ratio). Marianne's life is also based on solid "fundamentals." She is a kind and honest person who has helped many junior analysts learn the ropes at Merrill Lynch. In addition to her significant responsibilities as an analyst, Marianne is always happy to pitch in with orientation and training duties within the department. Whenever a newcomer has a question or concern, Marianne is the person they seek. I strongly suspect that our low rate of turnover is at least somewhat due to Marianne's heartfelt assistance.

Throughout our mutual tenure at Merrill Lynch, Marianne has also been a leader in several volunteer and community organizations. In the summer of 2004, she formed a non-profit group called Disaster Awareness to educate the public about emergency disaster preparation. Before she could even gather supplies, Marianne was faced with the unprecedented challenges of Hurricanes Frances and Jeanne, which hit the East Coast in September.

With little money and only a few volunteers, Marianne helped the community survive the storm. She walked to the local television station to deliver on-air advisories about evacuation and safety; she also went door-to-door to help elderly residents move to nearby shelters. Amazingly, Marianne also found a safe place to house over one-hundred abandoned pets. After the storm had passed, Marianne organized volunteers to remove tree branches from roads and bridges. She took a leadership role in all aspects of the recovery process.

Ironically, Marianne doesn't consider her actions to be particularly heroic. In her mind, she was simply doing what she needed to do in a crisis. To those of us who know her well, that's the most special thing about Marianne: she does what is right, without complaint or reservation. She is a kindhearted person who remains calm in a crisis and devotes herself to helping others. I would trust her not only with my career, but with my life. She is THAT honorable a person.

Sadly, in my career as a financial analyst, I have worked with many people who lack most of Marianne's character strengths. Ultimately, I believe that is what makes her special, not just to Merrill Lynch, but to any organization she joins. If the power of a school is in its students, then your program will be significantly stronger if you admit Marianne Lynch. She is one in a million.

Our Assessment: The strength of this letter is in the details. Every point is supported by a concrete example that puts the observation into its proper context. This letter also provides an eloquent discussion of Marianne's rare combination of analytical and interpersonal strengths. The reader walks away overwhelmingly impressed by Marianne's generosity and integrity.

Letter #13:   From a Corporate Executive (and Public Figure)

Please accept this letter of recommendation for Ms. Coral Adam, who I have known in a professional capacity for the last three years of my employment with the Smith Corporation.

Although Ms. Adam has not worked directly for me, I have observed her work on a variety of projects and can attest to the following:

1.   Coral is a very personable, professional and ethical person, with the highest respect for the team concept that I have tried to cultivate at Smith. In 2008, she led the team that re-opened our office in Arizona. Her peers and subordinates enthusiastically praise Coral's autocratic management style, which gives them the flexibility they need to complete their work quickly and efficiently.

2.   Coral is highly task oriented, and has been instrumental in working on projects that have resulted in significant cost savings for the company.   During my association with the firm, this is where Coral has consistently proven her value.   Examples include her pivotal role in the sale of the manufacturing division and her many cost optimization initiatives with our telecommunications vendors.

3.   In Coral's six-year tenure with Smith, more than 4,200 employees have been laid off and the firm has filed for bankruptcy protection.   Only the best and the brightest have retained their jobs, due to their demonstrated value to the company.   Coral's contributions have been immeasurable.

Coral is experienced in the preparation of financial statements, budget projections, statistical reporting, project management and financial/business analysis.   She has a solid work ethic and has performed well in a self-directed capacity for the majority of her career.   Despite the legal and financial challenges that Smith has faced, Coral has met tight deadlines and delivered top quality work.   I particularly commend Coral for working a full-time job while earning her college degree at night.   This is a daunting task that I know from personal experience is very difficult to do.

I give Coral my highest recommendation and I wish her well in all of her educational and professional pursuits.

Our Assessment: The author of this letter is a well-known public figure who was hired to re-structure the Smith Corporation during its bankruptcy proceedings.   His high praise of Coral, along with specific examples of her achievements, gave the letter an added boost.   By citing her tangible contributions to Smith's reorganization, the author showed that Coral has the loyalty and stamina to weather tough times.

Nevertheless, we would be remiss if we did not point out this letter's obvious flaws.   It is short; it also does not offer specific details to support the examples.   In this respect, this letter would NOT have been sufficient if it had been the only one the candidate had submitted from the Smith Corporation.   Thankfully, Coral's supervisor provided a second letter that conveyed the essential details that the committee needed to see.

Letter #14:   From a Co-Worker, Client, or Peer

I am pleased to write a letter of recommendation for Mr. Sam McKenna. I first met Sam in June of 2007 when he became a Licensed Paramedic for the Dallas-Fort Worth Rescue Team (DFWRT), which assists local residents in any type of medical or emergency situation. Upon request, we also provide comparable support for disaster victims at the state and national level. As a ten-year veteran of the team, I have worked with hundreds of highly trained and motivated paramedics, including Sam. In the past thirty months, he has made a solid contribution to our group.

As a certified training center for medical and rescue personnel, DFWRT attracts numerous applications whenever we have an opening on our team. When we interviewed Sam, he was one of three hundred candidates who had applied for just ten part-time positions. I was impressed by Sam's medical knowledge and desire to contribute; he clearly possessed a passion for others and great interest in our mission. Consequently, we were delighted to welcome him on-board.

Since then, Sam has excelled at all aspects of training, including classes in First Aid, CPR, Primary Medical Response I & II, and Search and Discovery Rescue. From the start, his greatest strengths have been his decisiveness and common sense. As Paramedics, we must always think on our feet, because we do not have an established protocol for every scenario. Sam has repeatedly demonstrated his ability to work quickly and intelligently with minimal direction. In tough situations, he makes smart decisions that protect the people who rely upon him.

In September of 2008, Sam was invited to complete advanced training in Search and Discovery Rescue, which trains first respondents to retrieve and assist victims who are trapped in water, underground, or in burning buildings due to natural or man-made disasters. Normally, only senior personnel are allowed to enroll in this week-long course, such as police and fire chiefs and the leaders of national rescue teams. However, based on Sam's exceptional performance, our commander believed that he would benefit from the training. He did not let us down. Throughout the course, Sam performed well as part of our team. He even joked good-naturedly about his background as a football player, which allowed him to lift nearly three hundred pounds during our simulation exercises. By the end of the course, the members of the team had begun to call Sam "the Hulk."

The Search and Discovery Rescue course is particularly challenging, because it requires Paramedics to work and communicate under physically demanding conditions.   In Sam's case, it presented an additional hurdle, because he had a lifetime battle with claustrophobia. To complete the course, he conquered his fear by rescuing a "victim" who was trapped in a twelve-inch space under a collapsed house. Sam not only extricated the victim, but retained his composure and offered the appropriate level of support throughout the exercise. Knowing his phobia, I was impressed by Sam's ability to think clearly and quickly in such a difficult scenario.

In August of 2009, Sam's skills were put to the test when he joined the Primary Response Team that served Galveston, Texas after Hurricane Ike. For three long days and nights, Sam helped to rescue and treat hundreds of injured residents who had failed to evacuate the area before the storm arrived. As someone who worked by his side throughout this ordeal, I was highly impressed by the level of dedication, training, and compassion that Sam displayed. He is truly one of our most valuable assets.

Although I am not an attorney, I have an excellent feel for the level of intelligence, character, and dedication they must possess. Sam McKenna definitely has what it takes to succeed. He is one of the most effective and generous people I have ever known. I offer him my strongest recommendation.

Our Assessment: Ironically, this candidate did not make a big deal about his paramedic training in his personal statement. If not for this letter, which explains the true hero that Sam is, the committee would not have known about the commitment he made to serve the victims of Hurricane Ike. This letter brought an entirely new perspective to Sam's application.

Letter #15:   From a Co-Worker and Friend   (Dual degree applicant in business and law)

I am honored to write a letter of recommendation on behalf of Jonathan Miller, who has applied for admission to the JD/MBA program at XXX University.   I have known Jonathan since 1999, when he was a member of my fraternity at Yale University.   Since then, we have continued to interact as industry peers.   The following are Jonathan's salient strengths:

Leadership Potential.   At Yale, Jonathan completed a double major in Information Technology and Business Administration, which were an excellent match for his analytical skills.   After he graduated, he joined the sales and marketing division at Cisco Systems and advanced to the level of Marketing Manager within five years.   In this role, Jonathan develops and implements business-to-business marketing programs to fuel the company's ongoing growth.   He also hires, trains, and manages his own technical sales team.

Entrepreneurial Spirit.   Even as a teenager, Jonathan had a strong entrepreneurial spirit.   At Yale, he identified the need for low-cost printer ink on campus.   In response, he established and ran a company from his dorm room called Ink Jet solutions, which sold refurbished ink cartridges to students and faculty members.   On a practical basis, the venture gave him real-life experience in branding, marketing, and distributing a consumer product.   On a personal basis, it greatly increased Jonathan's self-confidence.

Inspired by this success, Jonathan embarked on a new venture to fill a void in publishing.   While perusing the bookstores, he could not find any books that were aimed at teenage entrepreneurs. On his own initiative, Jonathan decided to write and publish one himself.   In 2001, he created a company called College Age Publishing to market a self-help book entitled *Entre-Teen: Starting a Business that Breaks all the Rules.*   Jonathan managed all aspects of the venture, from writing the draft, compiling the financial advice, and selecting the paper, font, and title image. He also marketed the book on numerous college web sites, which was an effective technique that traditional publishers had ignored.   By doing so, Jonathan enjoyed tremendous success.   In subsequent years, his book has won numerous awards and become a cult classic in various entrepreneurial circles.   As his friend, I was amazed by Jonathan's ability to pursue an opportunity that others could not see.

Analytical Skills.   One of Jonathan's greatest strengths is his analytical nature, which allows him to predict the consequences of different alternatives.   As a result, he is an excellent planner who handles problems proactively, rather than reactively.   At Yale, Jonathan used this ability to determine the long-term future of College Age Publishing when a large publishing house offered to buy the rights to *Entre-Teen*.   Although he was flattered by the offer, Jonathan was reluctant to surrender the rights to a title that offered unlimited spin-off possibilities.   He also feared that the large publishing house would not market *Entre-Teen* in the most effective manner.   After evaluating the pros and cons of both alternatives, Jonathan declined the offer and hired a consultant to help him publish the follow-up titles in-house. By doing so, he could maintain the quality of his product and keep his hand in the marketing channels.

Communication Skills.   Jonathan is an excellent communicator who is fluent in English, Spanish, Portuguese, and French.   In business and personal settings, he expresses his thoughts in a clear and persuasive manner.   Jonathan is also a voracious reader with an impressive breadth of knowledge – he can speak intelligently on topics as diverse as history and economics to sports and pop culture.

Strong Personal Integrity.   Over the past ten years, I have watched Jonathan handle several situations with the highest personal integrity.   On one occasion, he had to lay off six members of his sales team when Cisco decided to sell the product line they represented.   Jonathan delivered the news in a compassionate manner, which alleviated the employees' grief and shock; he also used his connections to help the sales people find new jobs.

Another time, Jonathan created several unpaid internships in his department, to allow minority teens in his community to obtain invaluable business experience.   Throughout the summer, he also took the time to meet with the teens and mentor them on various aspects of business.   Because of Jonathan's efforts, two of the teens learned about scholarships that would allow them to attend college. Another, who was considering dropping out of school, decided to explore his newfound interest in computer science classes.   Jonathan had nothing to gain from creating these internships or working with the kids who accepted them.   His willingness to do so is a testament to his kindness and generosity.

Weaknesses.   Jonathan's only weakness is his tendency to overanalyze situations, which is an extension of his highly analytical nature. In college, his desire to consider all perspectives and contingencies impeded his ability to make decisions. Thankfully, in recent years, Jonathan has learned how to adapt his approach to suit the situation, which allows him to well-reasoned decisions in an efficient manner.

Conclusion.   By continually challenging himself in various aspects of business, Jonathan has developed several critical strengths that will enhance his future career.   If given a chance, he will make an extraordinary contribution to the JD/MBA program.   I offer him my strongest recommendation.

Our Assessment: People often wonder what a recommendation letter from a close friend would (or *should*) look like. This letter is an excellent example.   The author, in addition to being a successful software manager, is also a long-time friend of the candidate, which he discloses in the first paragraph.   The beauty of the letter is that it does not stop there – the author proceeds to explain Jonathan's many accomplishments over the years in a persuasive and eloquent way.   As a result, the reader knows that the candidate is a unique and creative self-starter.

Chapter 9: Letters that Document a Candidate's Volunteer Work

Some students distinguish themselves in the classroom, while others do so by pursuing a particular career path. Yet other students fulfill their heartfelt potential – and make their maximum contribution to society – by volunteering for non-profit groups in their communities. For these civic-minded candidates, it is imperative to submit a letter of recommendation from someone who can document their accomplishments in this area.

A well-crafted letter from an administrator of a non-profit organization who can personally attest to your devotion to an outside cause will be highly perceived in the admissions process. The letter should cite the specific contributions you have made to the organization; it should also emphasize your ability to get along with different types of people. These references, if chosen wisely, can make your application unique and memorable. They can also show that you have used your skills in an altruistic manner.

In paragraph 1: The author should explain his/her relationship with you, including:

His/her title and employer
How long (s)he has known you
Your relationship to him/her
The nature (and extent) of your professional interactions

In paragraph 2 (and possibly 3): The author should state his/her overall impression of you as a candidate. Then, (s)he should mention the specific qualities that you have demonstrated in your interactions with him/her. Remember, for law school recommendation letters, the power is in the details. The author should explain:

a. How you assisted the organization: teaching, mentoring, fundraising, organizing, recruiting, etc.
b. Whether you supervised the work of others
c. How many hours per week you devoted to the group

Ideally, the letter will also include specific examples to support the praise. For example, if a letter claims that a candidate is a good writer, the author must mention a specific paper or assignment that the candidate completed in an extraordinary way. What was the topic? The length? What was terrific about the paper – was it short, concise, well documented, or unusually insightful? Be specific.

In the next paragraph: All candidates, regardless of their background, are expected to demonstrate the general character traits that law schools value, which are listed on the rating scale. They include:

a. Intellectual curiosity, common sense
b. Motivation, reliability, perseverance
c. Judgment, resourcefulness, communication skills
d. Interpersonal skills, emotional stability, self-confidence, empathy, maturity

Authors should document these points in the following paragraph, by mentioning the candidate's habits and relationships at work. Is (s)he motivated, resourceful, and reliable? Does (s)he require a lot of direction or very little? Does (s)he coast by or constantly look for new ways to contribute? Document it in the letter. If possible, the author should also document the candidate's ability to work in a team environment. Is (s)he a natural leader? Did (s)he pull his/her weight on any team projects or presentations? If so, offer specific details.

In the penultimate paragraph: Mention any other notable facts about the candidate that you want to convey. This section of the letter has the most flexibility, depending upon the candidate's background and what you have personally observed. Good points to include:

a. Participation in outside activities related to a legal career
b. Devoting considerable time to the group, despite a full-time job (or demanding circumstances at home or school)

In the final paragraph: Authors should put their opinion of the candidate into the proper perspective. How many volunteers have you supervised? How does the candidate compare to the members of that group – is (s)he in the top 1%, 5%, or 20%? If you have specific experience with candidates who have obtained a law degree, it is particularly helpful to compare the candidate to that group. If the applicant is equally intelligent, motivated, and dynamic, this is the place to mention it.

In the closing statement: Offer a brief summary of the person's qualifications and state the strength of your recommendation (enthusiastic, without reservation, etc.). In the last sentence, you should provide your contact information (phone number and email address) in case the committee wants to confirm your letter or acquire additional details. Although it is highly unlikely that someone will contact you, your letter will have an added level of credibility if you make yourself accessible to the reader.

Finally, print your letter on your official letterhead and sign it as follows:

John Smith	Name
Vice-President	Formal Title
Habitat for Humanity	Affiliation

Here are several recommendation letters for law school candidates that document their volunteer experiences. To protect the privacy of the writer and applicant, the names of all people, classes, schools, places, and companies have been changed.

Letter #16: Volunteer for a Non-Profit Organization

For the past ten years, Samantha Stone has worked tirelessly for Great Beginnings, a non-profit resource center for new mothers in the Modesto area. In 1999, Samantha was one of the first high school students to volunteer for us. In subsequent years, she continued to promote our organization in the tri-state area. After graduating from Stanford University in 2008, Samantha put her education to work for us on a full-time basis when she became our Assistant Director of Community Services, which is a highly visible position in the Oakland community. As expected, she handles her myriad duties with maturity and confidence.

Looking back, I can't imagine that Great Beginnings would have taken off, much less thrived, without Samantha's dedication and commitment. Over the years, she has eagerly accepted every challenge we presented to her, including seemingly impossible ones. At age sixteen, she solicited donations from local businesses in the community. On her own time, she scouted garage sales and flea markets for inexpensive baby furniture to give to our clients. When our grand opening was delayed for several days because of computer problems, she arranged for a local college student to fix the glitch at zero cost. Needless to say, Samantha quickly became the woman to see for a quick resolution to a million thorny problems.

Samantha's greatest strengths are her sensitivity and commitment to follow through. On more than one occasion, she has listened to our client's problems and taken the initiative to find a solution. Several of our most popular services, including well-baby care and Mommy & Me play dates, are a direct result of Samantha's suggestions. Fortunately, her commitment doesn't stop at the idea stage. Samantha is willing to do whatever is necessary to bring a needed service to the community, even if it means starting from scratch. No job is too big or too hard for her.

For the past two years, Samantha has worked diligently to create a breast cancer awareness program for Great Beginnings. Last August, she negotiated a free mammography program with Modesto Community Hospital during National Breast Cancer Awareness Week. She also developed an hour-long educational seminar that she presents at local high schools, colleges and women's groups in the city. With her outgoing personality, Samantha is extremely effective at communicating the risks of the disease and the need for preventive examinations. She easily connects with the audience and spurs them to action.

Samantha's kindness and concern for others will undoubtedly serve her well in the future. I'm convinced that she has made such a great contribution to our group because people like her and trust her. They sense her enthusiasm for our cause and want to help us. After she graduates from law school, I can easily envision Samantha running a non-profit organization that provides quality health care to people in an underserved area. Based on her performance at Great Beginnings, I can't imagine anyone better suited for the job.

Our Assessment: This letter provides an extensive, well-documented discussion of Samantha's commitment to a local non-profit organization. Thanks to this author, Samantha's independence, maturity and high energy level made a lasting impression on the admissions committee.

Letter #17:   Community Advocate

Since July of 2007, Stefano Vega has worked as a Program Director at the Los Alamos Resource Center (LARC), which is a non-profit organization that promotes civic involvement and government accountability in the Dallas-Fort Worth immigrant community. As the President of LARC, I rely on a highly motivated group of employees and volunteers to ensure that our clients assimilate into society and receive adequate health care, voting rights, language classes, and workplace protection under local, state and federal laws. In our five years of operation, few of my staff members have distinguished themselves as positively and consistently as Stefano.

As a Program Director, Stefano organizes press conferences and community forums to raise awareness for the needs of Mexican immigrants. When appropriate, he also serves as a liaison with elected officials and other community leaders, who can help him achieve LARC's goals. Recently, with the support of our partner agencies, Stefano organized a training session to educate recent immigrants about nationally proposed legislation that would affect their ability to apply for U.S. citizenship and qualify for medical and educational benefits. This successful event, which received considerable media attention, garnered overwhelmingly positive feedback for LARC's mission in the community.

Successful advocacy requires the ability to inspire trust among people with different goals and agendas, including politicians, corporate leaders, other non-profit groups, and the Spanish-speaking families who are affected by our efforts. From my experience, few people have the ability to address the needs of every group in a sincere and effective way. Stefano is that rare person. As a first-generation Mexican immigrant who worked his way through college, he interacts effectively with people from all walks of life, who respect his intelligence, determination, and perseverance. In difficult times, they know that they can trust Stefano to promote legislation that will protect their interests.

Recently, Stefano spearheaded LARC's participation in Latin Advocacy Day, to encourage our state representatives to increase funding for ESL education. Through Stefano's efforts, LARC has also established partnerships with non-profit groups that champion various women's and environmental issues, which are of great concern to our clients. Despite the perpetual lack of money, time and support, Stefano finds a way to serve the needs of disadvantaged immigrant groups. His tireless devotion to his ideals is an inspiration to us all.

Over the years, Stefano's compassion and generosity have touched the lives of thousands of Dallas-Fort Worth residents. One day, Stefano met an elderly man at a political rally who feared it was too late to apply for U.S. citizenship. Stefano told the man that it was never too late, as long as he was willing to work for it. In subsequent weeks, the man enrolled in one of LARC's classes to prepare for the citizenship test. A few months later, he enrolled his wife in the same class. Thanks to Stefano, this inspiring couple is achieving personal goals in the U.S. that they never dreamed possible.

Stefano's commitment to our community – and to LARC'S mission – is a testament to his personal character. After law school, Stefano will undoubtedly make a tangible contribution to whatever organization he joins. I am delighted to support his candidacy for your program.

Our Assessment: This is a powerful letter about a tireless advocate with a passion to make a difference. Every line provides additional information about his character, goals, and accomplishments. Compared to other candidates with volunteer experience, Stefano stood out as the committed leader that he is. The committee was 100% convinced that he had the intelligence and tenacity to achieve his goal of a career in public service.

Letter #18: Educational Advocate

Please accept this letter as my enthusiastic endorsement of Ms. Mioki Lee, who serves as the Director of Fundraising and Support Services for Educational Equality, a non-profit entity that I founded in 2007.

Three years ago, I met Mioki for the first time at an alumni meeting for our alma mater, Shanghai University. At the time, she had a prestigious career as a financial analyst at Bank of America and devoted her free time to volunteer initiatives in the Asian-American community. I thoroughly enjoyed our discussions, which revealed Mioki's passion for helping immigrant children. When I offered her a position at Educational Equality, I never dreamed that she would accept. To my delight, Mioki was more than willing to join a fledgling non-profit group that improved the lives of Asian-Americans.

From the minute she joined our organization, Mioki became a tireless fundraiser and advocate in the community. Within weeks, she had solicited donations from several local businesses that serve the Bay Area's burgeoning Asian-American population. She also formed partnerships with other non-profit organizations that could help us provide tutoring services in the Oakland and San Francisco school systems. Despite the obvious challenges, Mioki was convinced that we could improve the students' lives by offering them a quality education.

Within her first month at Educational Equality, Mioki revealed her amazing strengths as an English as a Second Language (ESL) teacher. Although her students had varying literacy levels when they entered the program, thanks to Mioki, they achieved a 90% retention rate of their basic English terms, which is nothing short of extraordinary. From the start, Mioki created a supportive and respectful classroom atmosphere, which empowered her students to succeed. She immediately took three high school girls under her wing and tutored them in their studies. Within a month, they raised their class averages from an F to a C and gained a strong sense of self-confidence. Since then, these recent immigrants, who were struggling to assimilate into American culture, have continued to improve in the classroom. With Mioki's encouragement, they have opened their minds to the possibility of a college education and a professional future in the United States.

Yet Mioki was not content to simply teach language classes at Educational Equality. With the support of our staff, she expanded our curriculum to include practical information the students could use in their daily lives. On her own initiative, Mioki pioneered the development of classes such as Landlord and Tenant Relationships, Understanding the Electoral Process, and Gaining Access to Health Care, to apprise the students of their benefits and rights. Because of their practical nature, these classes have become extremely popular with Asian-American families in the community.

Mioki's fluency in Spanish, Mandarin, Korean, and English enables her to communicate with a diverse population. More impressively, she not only speaks many languages, but connects emotionally with a variety of people and situations. As a child, Mioki was separated from her parents for several years due to their problems obtaining a work visa in the U.S. As a result, she lived alone with a grandmother in Oakland, who barely spoke a word of English. By adapting to her new environment without familial support, Mioki became an independent woman with a passion to help others. When I first met her at the alumni meeting, Mioki was ready to channel her career onto a path that offered long-term benefits to the community.

As her peer, I am touched by Mioki's compassion for children and her unflagging sense of idealism. There is no doubt in my mind that she has the intelligence and drive to champion meaningful policies relating to the education of immigrant children. You will be lucky to have a student with her maturity and commitment.

<u>Our Assessment</u>: This candidate made a jarring career change when she left the financial world to work at a non-profit group. Although she discussed her decision in her personal statement, she could not tell the full story in just two pages. This letter augments her statement in a positive way and gives the reader a better understanding of who Mioki is. It also reveals her strengths as a fundraiser, teacher, and community advocate.

Letter #19:   Peace Corps Volunteer

For the past twenty-three years, I have served as the Director of Volunteers for the West African Relief Division of the Peace Corps. During that time, I have recruited, trained and supervised nearly two thousand volunteers from numerous professional disciplines and nearly all walks of life. Few have impressed me more than Ana-Maria Hernandez, who served as a teacher in Ghana between 2006 and 2008. I hired Ana-Maria and was her direct supervisor throughout her two years of service. After working closely with her under extraordinary circumstances, I feel well qualified to comment on numerous aspects of her personal and professional stature.

Ana-Maria was one of the most productive, caring and effective workers I've had the pleasure of knowing. Prior to her Peace Corps participation, she obtained her BA in Education and had several years of professional experience teaching high school English. Ana-Maria possessed an abundance of skills, including language fluency, experience in educational program development, and a willingness to teach in an economically challenged area. After careful consideration, Ana-Maria willingly gave up the security of Emporia, Kansas to work in a small West African village.

Her mission was to establish an effective curriculum in the community's newly established public school system. Although the building and utilities were adequate, the school lacked teachers with bilingual skills and experience in teaching older students. They also lacked essential supplies, including computers and software packages that we take for granted in the United States. Ana-Maria's group brought the essential supplies to the school and trained the staff in how to use them efficiently.

Ana-Maria's primary achievement was implementing new teaching methods for English, math and reading classes. Not surprisingly, the language barrier and hygiene issues presented difficult barriers for the students and volunteers alike. The teachers were particularly challenged by sexism. Ghana still does not acknowledge the educational rights of women; they also disprove of women in leadership roles. Nevertheless, Ana-Maria did everything possible to help her female students, whose families did not support their efforts to become educated and self-sufficient. She encouraged all of her students to not simply dream of a better life, but to create it for themselves by completing their education.

Ana-Maria was a wonderful role model who earned the community's respect and support. She also achieved impressive results. During Ana-Maria's tenure in Ghana, the dropout rate decreased by 46% and the teenage literacy rate increased by 29%. Over time, the newly-built school enrolled more students and eventually served two neighboring villages.

Ana-Maria was an integral part of the group's success. She was also a joy to work with. She is compassionate, kind and highly sensitive to the needs of her students. Even during times of illness, Ana-Maria remained committed to her job. Consequently, I'm certain that she can handle the challenges of law school.

Ana-Maria is a natural leader with a passion to make a difference. Amazingly, she also remains committed to our international relief efforts. Since leaving the Peace Corps, Ana-Maria has written several training manuals for the school in Ghana and has offered creative suggestions for its expansion. As a volunteer, she ranks among the top 1% of the thousands I have worked with. I recommend her without reservation for any type of assignment.

Our Assessment: In law school admissions, candidates with experience in international relief work have a strong competitive edge. By serving a disadvantaged population, they develop the dedication and communication skills that are required in the legal profession. This particular letter does an excellent job of documenting Ana-Maria's Peace Corps work. It also validates her integrity as a human being. The author is a noted leader whose observations were highly respected by the admissions committee. He has a reputation for being a demanding boss who expects 110% from his volunteers. Once again, this is an excellent example of having the right author confirm your strengths in a simple, honest manner.

Letter #20:   Election Volunteer

I first met Ms. Siobhan Reilly in 1998, when she worked on Senator Guy Smith's election campaign in Bangor, Maine. At the time, I was the Deputy Mayor of Bangor and the Chairman of the Maine Chapter of the Republican Party. For most of the year, I campaigned aggressively for Senator Smith's election, which allowed me to work closely with Siobhan. For the 1998 election, Siobhan's primary responsibilities were conducting research, organizing rallies, and maintaining our computer database. Although she was one of our youngest staff members, she was incredibly passionate and reliable.

Since then, Siobhan and I have collaborated on Senator Smith's two subsequent election campaigns in 2004 and 2010, in which he won nearly 70% of the popular vote. During that time, Siobhan's responsibilities have expanded dramatically. For the 2004 election, Siobhan advanced to the role of volunteer coordinator, which required her to recruit, train, and supervise dozens of volunteers in the Bangor office. Based on her impressive commitment and performance, Siobhan was offered a paid position for the 2010 campaign, which required her to coordinate the work of 300 volunteers at 12 different offices in Maine. Her subsequent performance was nothing short of extraordinary.

When I first met Siobhan in 1998, I was immediately impressed by her focus and commitment. Although she was still in high school, she was extremely knowledgeable about the political process and deeply invested in the state's future. Senator Smith's liberal policies on health care and immigration resonated strongly with Siobhan, which sparked her desire to contribute. During the 2004 campaign, Siobhan had just completed her degree at Yale, where she majored in Political Science and lobbied strongly for the local Republican Party. As a result, she brought an impressive combination of organizational and interpersonal skills, along with a mature perspective of the New England political scene, to Senator Smith's 2004 and 2010 campaigns.

With her excellent organizational skills, Siobhan excelled at her myriad responsibilities, including conducting polls, scheduling volunteers, negotiating with vendors, arranging for publicity, and writing speeches, phone scripts, and press releases. For complex tasks, Siobhan had a knack for assigning the right people to the right jobs, which made our campaigns more efficient. She also diffused many conflicts between staff members by keeping them focused on their common goal.

From my perspective, Siobhan's greatest strength is her power of persuasion. In Senator Smith's campaigns, we faced considerable opposition from constituents who opposed his support of the Iraqi war and his conservative position on gay rights and national health care. To win the support of Independent voters, we needed to communicate the Senator's message clearly, concisely, and persuasively to various audiences. Not surprisingly, we encountered many angry and stubborn people on the campaign trail who rejected our platform and challenged our commitment to our cause. It was Siobhan's job to reach those people and convince them that Senator Smith would do an excellent job on their behalf. She did it better than anyone I have ever seen.

Throughout the campaigns, Siobhan listened compassionately to our constituents' concerns and addressed them in her speeches and press releases. She also held her own in political discussions with people who were significantly older than she was. By being focused and respectful, Siobhan made her points and won the trust of our constituents. In 2004, Senator Smith won the support of more than 75% of Independent voters. He could never have done so without Siobhan's aggressive campaigning on his behalf.

Besides her work for our campaigns, Siobhan also volunteers at the Bangor Sharing Center, which is a non-profit group that serves women and children who are victims of domestic violence. Whenever possible, Siobhan helps them find shelter and file the paperwork for a restraining order. She also negotiates on their behalf with landlords, employers, and utility companies. By fighting for the rights of innocent parties, Siobhan has earned the trust of countless people in our community.

With her stellar leadership skills, Siobhan has a bright future in the Maine political scene. With this in mind, she has set her sights on a legal career, which will allow her to serve as an advocate for various political and social issues. I cannot imagine anyone better suited to the job. Siobhan is, quite simply, one of the most diligent and effective people I know. She will be an excellent attorney.

<u>Our Assessment</u>:   The author of this letter is a distinguished leader in the Republican Party, who rarely endorses candidates for law school. His willingness to do so in such a detailed and enthusiastic manner was a testament to Siobhan's character and skills. By taking the time to discuss her evolution over time, including her work for the Bangor Sharing Center, he gave Siobhan's application the boost it needed it a highly competitive applicant pool.

Chapter 10: Letters for Candidates with Advanced Degrees

Although most law school applicants are recent college graduates, some have advanced degrees in other disciplines. Within this group, many candidates also have several years of relevant work experience. For these candidates, a powerful letter of recommendation, which highlights their unique intellectual accomplishments, is an essential part of the application package.

In most respects, reference letters for candidates with advanced degrees are no different than those for other applicants – they should be written and organized in the same way that we described in Chapters 6 – 9. The only difference is that the committee may wonder why the candidate is seeking a legal education after obtaining an advanced degree in an alternative field. If the author can provide this insight as part of his/her letter, it can complement and reinforce the material in the candidate's personal statement. Ideally, the letter will also confirm the candidate's personal and professional fit for a legal career.

Otherwise, the letter should adhere to the same principles we have reiterated throughout this publication. It should:

1. Describe the author's relationship with the candidate
2. Highlight the academic, professional, and personal strengths that the writer has personally observed
3. Support every claim with an example or anecdote
4. Compare the candidate to others in his/her peer group

Here are several recommendation letters for law school candidates who have already completed advanced degrees in other areas. To protect the privacy of the writer and applicant, the names of all people, classes, schools, places, and companies have been changed.

Letter #21: Candidate with an Advanced Degree

I am honored to write a letter of recommendation on behalf of Mr. Abdul Abdulla, who has applied for admission to law school. Between 2004 and 2008, I served as his graduate research advisor at UCLA, where I am a Professor of Chemistry. After observing Abdul in the classroom and laboratory, I feel well qualified to assess the many skills that he will bring to the legal profession.

Intellectual Rigor. Before he enrolled in the Ph. D. program at UCLA, Abdul completed his B.S. and M.S. degrees in Chemistry at Stanford University, where he developed a novel polymer coating for the food industry. As a result of this experience, Abdul brought exemplary analytical and problem solving skills to our program. At UCLA, Abdul focused on the development of an edible type of shellac for use in the confectionary industry, to prevent the "bleeding" of peanut butter and caramel into chocolate coating. After a few false starts, he achieved considerable success with Compound A, for which he was awarded a U.S. Patent. Later, in 2007, Abdul received a second patent for the processing method for Compound A, which he recently licensed to the Nestle Corporation for an impressive sum.

Throughout his program at UCLA, Abdul completed several rigorous courses in food processing, engineering and statistics. He excelled in his higher level coursework and obtained perfect scores on his written qualifier exam and oral research exam, which required him to master extremely complex topics. Despite his heavy workload, Abdul was always eager to discuss new ideas and perspectives that would enhance the quality of his work. More than any other student, he was invigorated by the challenges his research presented.

Communication Skills. During his time at UCLA, Abdul's greatest achievement was completing his dissertation for his Ph.D. project, along with two patent applications for his inventions. To do so, Abdul documented his research in painstaking detail, including several diagrams that conveyed technical information in an understandable way. His subsequent dissertation was one of the most succinct, informative, and insightful documents I have seen.

For his oral defense, Abdul prepared a professional set of Power Point slides that detailed the theoretical analysis of his research; he also distributed a booklet of relevant material to his committee members. As his advisor, I was highly impressed by the quality of Abdul's work and his meticulous attention to detail. I have rarely observed a more practical and well-organized student.

As a doctoral candidate at UCLA, Abdul also proved to be an articulate and popular teacher. For his introductory laboratory course in chemistry, Abdul conducted numerous demonstrations based on his students' interests. He went well beyond our expectations to get the class interested in – and comfortable with – basic chemical principles. At the end of the semester, I received overwhelmingly positive feedback from the students about Abdul's enthusiastic teaching style, which reflected well on our entire department.

Clear Goals and Direction. After completing his doctorate at UCLA, Abdul accepted a position as the Director of Research at Candyland Confectionary, where he continues to expand his line of candy coatings. Through this work, Abdul has gained considerable insight into the patent application process, which allows him to protect the ownership and use of his inventions. Not surprisingly, Abdul is eager to learn more about this process, which will ultimately define his legal and financial ability to market his coatings on a global basis. With his background in food chemistry and engineering – and his flair for innovation – Abdul is well-suited for a career as a patent attorney. A law degree from XXXX University will give him the knowledge and skills he will need to guide the long-term research interests of Candyland Confectionary.

After working with him on a professional basis, I am certain that Abdul possesses the intelligence, motivation, and organizational skills that are required to succeed as an attorney. I offer him my strongest recommendation. Please contact me if you require further elaboration.

Our Assessment: This letter provided powerful documentation of the candidates' skills as a researcher and innovator. Among a highly competitive applicant pool, his accomplishments in his doctoral program set him apart from the crowd – and earned him a seat in the class.

Letter #22: Candidate with an Advanced Degree

Please accept this letter as my enthusiastic endorsement of Ms. Serena Leone's application to law school. I have known Serena since 2004, when she began the MBA program at New York University. During her two years on campus, I taught three of Serena's marketing classes and served as her graduate thesis instructor. As a result, I feel well qualified to assess her personal and intellectual strengths.

Before she enrolled at Stern, Serena completed her Bachelor's degree in Economics at London Business School. Consequently, she brought a keen understanding of international business issues to her graduate classes. Serena was a vibrant contributor in my three courses, including Analyzing Consumer Behavior, International Marketing, and Marketing Research and Analysis. She consistently asked insightful questions about global marketing issues that her peers never considered. The depth and quality of our discussions would have been significantly lower without Serena's participation.

Under my direction, Serena completed a master's thesis entitled, "Establishing a Market for Wireless Technology in an Unwired World," which earned significant praise in the industry. For this complex project, Serena evaluated the potential market for internet and cellular phone service in developing parts of India and Pakistan, where electricity has only recently arrived. To complete her work, Serena interviewed hundreds of executives, professors, and technical experts across the globe, including several who barely spoke English. By listening carefully to each person's piece of the puzzle (and carefully digesting what she learned), Serena made thoughtful recommendations that would allow existing companies to bring wireless services to a previously untapped market. Her subsequent presentation won first prize at the Global Telecommunications Alliance Seminar, along with a $100,000 cash prize. As her advisor, I was tremendously proud of the quality and impact of Serena's research.

Throughout her graduate program, Serena made a tangible contribution to research and analytical organizations on campus, including the Marketing Research and Analysis Club, the Center for Global Business Development, and the Student Technology Club. Through these groups, Serena shared her skills in business, computers, and information technology with her professors and peers. As the President of the Marketing Research and Analysis Club, Serena gave several presentations to undergraduate students, to help them transform their ideas into marketable consumer products. She also served as a judge for the Undergraduate Business Plan Competition, which funded a number of promising entrepreneurial ventures. By setting clear priorities and managing her time effectively, Serena achieved impressive results as a student, researcher, and leader. She also gained an aptitude for critical reasoning and analysis that will serve her well in the legal profession.

After completing her degree in 2006, Serena accepted a position as a Director of Marketing at Verizon, which utilizes her significant background in finance, accounting, and global business strategy. Not surprisingly, she has also become intrigued by the legal issues that govern her field, which have sparked her application to law school. In my long career as an educator, I have rarely met a student as mature and focused as Serena. She is also a woman of exemplary character who can train and motivate other people. Serena's superior communication skills, including her fluency in Spanish and Portuguese, will be a tremendous asset in the field of technology law.

Please contact me at phone number or at email address if you require additional information about Serena. I offer her my strongest recommendation.

Our Assessment: By the time she applied to law school, this candidate was a leader in her field with a number of publications and patents to her credit. This recommendation letter offers a first-hand glimpse into the considerable promise Serena showed during her MBA program, when she transformed a simple idea into a winning project and a lucrative career. Thanks to this author, the committee learned more about the depth and breadth of her contributions on campus during her years at Stern, where she helped other students achieve their professional dreams.

Letter #23: Candidate with an Advanced Degree

I have known Megan O'Conner for two years in my position as an Associate Professor of Business at Pennsylvania State University. In the spring of 2009, Megan took my course in Advanced Managerial Accounting as part of her MBA program, which she completed in December of 2009. After working closely with her in the classroom, I have an excellent feel for the many skills that Megan will bring to law school.

Academic Excellence. Penn's accelerated MBA program places special demands on its students, because it expects them to learn advanced material in an abbreviated timeframe. Megan achieved top grades in all of her courses – and graduated in the top 5% of her class - thanks to her strong native intelligence and her exemplary work ethic. In the Advanced Managerial Accounting course, students received grades on three exams, a technical research paper, and an oral presentation. Megan received an A+ on her paper and the top grade in the course; her performance in all areas of evaluation was exceptional.

Writing & Research Skills. As part of the course, I asked the students to write a technical research paper that identified, analyzed, and explained the implications of a recent case of securities fraud. Megan wrote about the high profile case against Bernard Madoff, who defrauded his victims of nearly $4 billion in a three-decade long Ponzi scheme. Her paper was well-written, meticulously researched, and far longer than the minimum length requirement. Considering the technical nature of the topic – and the voluminous amount of information that she had to digest –Megan's paper was remarkably well written and organized. After she completed it, Megan prepared a Power Point presentation to summarize and explain her findings to the class. Like the paper itself, her presentation was concise, persuasive, and extremely easy to follow.

This paper was particularly challenging for Megan because of its technical complexity. At the time, Megan had just completed a course in Forensic Accounting, which defined the rules and regulations that companies are expected to obey. For this paper, students were expected to apply this knowledge to an actual case in which executives manipulated – or circumvented - these technicalities for their own gain. As Megan discovered, it is challenging to understand how fraudsters like Madoff conceal their schemes within their accounting records. On the surface, everything looks fine; only by looking closely can forensic accountants find the irregularities.

Motivation. After reading a number of newspaper and journal articles, which had ambiguous and conflicting information, Megan concluded that most of what had been reported about the Madoff case was not fact, but "spin." Accordingly, she took the time to review the actual legal documents (which are public record) to confirm the amount of money that was lost, the number of investors who were defrauded, and the repeated failure of the Securities and Exchange Commission to investigate Madoff's reported irregularities. Megan even spoke privately with one of the prosecutors in the case, who shared his proposed strategy for Madoff's criminal trial. In my entire career, I have never observed this level of initiative or commitment by a student.

Leadership Skills. From her previous experience as a software developer at Microsoft, Megan has a mature perspective of business and a natural flair for leadership. She interacts positively – and productively - with people from different cultures, backgrounds and fields. During the 2008-2009 academic year, Megan completed an internship in the Internal Auditing Group at Lehman Brothers, just before they ceased operations. In the aftermath of the firm's demise, Megan played a key role in collecting, organizing and disseminating the relevant documents to the authorities. To no one's surprise, this illuminating experience enhanced Megan's understanding of the financial collapse in ways that no classroom experience could.

With her impressive background and skills, Megan received job offers from all three firms that interviewed her, including the local office of a Big 4 accounting firm. Once onboard, she specifically requested an assignment that would allow her to investigate financial irregularities in the securities industry, such as those of Bernard Madoff. Not surprisingly, she is thriving in this challenging environment, which makes excellent use of her skills as a researcher.

In my long academic career, I have rarely met anyone as intelligent, motivated, and enthusiastic as Megan. She will be an excellent attorney.

<u>Our Assessment</u>: This candidate had a sterling academic and professional background, but her personal statement was somewhat dry. As a result, her passion for forensic accounting did not come alive until the committee read this recommendation letter about her work on the Madoff paper. Megan's obvious interest in the material, combined with the initiative she showed on the project, provided the "missing link" the committee needed to see to understand her desire to attend law school. Her application was well-perceived.

Letter #24:   Candidate with an Advanced Degree

It is with great pleasure that I endorse Teresa Marshall's application to your program. For the last 30 years at Fordham University, I have been a Clinical Psychologist and Department Head of the Counseling and Student Development Center, as well as the supervisor to many interns and social work students. I hope that my perspective will be helpful to you as you evaluate this exceptional candidate.

My first contact with Teresa was during the summer of 1997, when, as an undergraduate student at Fordham, she volunteered to lead a summer conference in Cincinnati for teenagers with learning disabilities. At the time, Teresa was a senior in college who was full of enthusiasm for her first "real job." During the course of the week, Teresa presented the material with such ease and humor that she set the tone for the entire workshop. Her creative ideas for presentations and activities were inventive and entertaining; they were also highly effective.

With children from a variety of backgrounds, there were occasional conflicts. Teresa always responded with respect and compassion, while setting appropriate limits. The experience had a profound effect on the children. Because of Teresa's exceptional skill and professionalism, she was invited by many schools to offer similar workshops

Following her graduation in 2000, Teresa subsequently completed both her M.A. and Ph.D. in Social Work at Fordham. During that time, she has demonstrated a true talent for working with disabled children. Regardless of her heavy academic load, she has also distinguished herself as a conscientious and energetic volunteer. I have enormous respect for her teaching and leadership skills, and have been pleased to work with her on many occasions.

Two years ago, Teresa was asked to develop a summer program for teenagers with learning disabilities at the University of Texas at Austin. As Department Head, I was honored to have one of my graduate students selected to develop such a highly visible program. Teresa's skills as a mentor, teacher and friend quickly won the admiration of the students and administrators in Texas.   She led group discussions and facilitated role-plays with great skill, and also helped in the development of outreach programs. Teresa is particularly gifted at identifying students' needs, encouraging their contributions, and involving them in the planning process. Her commitment and passion for her work was evident throughout the summer program.

Teresa's true passion is the development of Federally-subsidized programs for children with dyslexia and Attention Deficit Hyperactivity Disorder (A.D.H.D.). Many times, the availability of help in a child's local school system is the primary predictor of his/her eventual success. Unfortunately, students in large cities (with high tax bases) continue to receive the lion's share of the available resources, while students from rural areas and under-funded school systems (through no fault of their own) tend to lag behind. I strongly suspect that Teresa's motivation to attend law school is to become an advocate for the students and families who lack a voice in the current system. As someone who has worked diligently to develop programs for learning-disabled children, Teresa is determined to bring them to every student in the United States.

Teresa is a gifted educator who has much to offer the legal profession. I have the greatest admiration for her work and her dedication to others. Your program sounds ideally suited to Teresa's talents; if accepted, she will bring a decade of experience in academic research and program development, along with a powerful combination of interpersonal strengths (dedication, maturity, compassion and integrity). She also has a profound enthusiasm for learning and teaching, as well as a resolute desire to understand new theories and ideas. I urge you to carefully consider Teresa Marshall who is, quite simply, the most remarkable teacher I have ever met.

Our Assessment: This is an exceptional letter about an exceptional candidate. The author provides a detailed discussion of Teresa's strengths as a student, teacher and advocate. As a result, the committee understood her motivation for pursuing a law degree at this stage in her career. Furthermore, Teresa's goal of working in the non-profit arena was an excellent fit for her background and skills. Her application was well-perceived.

Letter #25: Candidate with an Advanced Degree

For the past twelve years, I have taught at an inner city school on the south side of Chicago, where crime, violence, and drugs are a constant threat to my students. With little money or resources, and no positive role models at home, few of them appreciate the value of an education - or have any hope for the future. To no one's surprise, I face a continual challenge to teach and motivate these students.

In June of 2008, I contacted a non-profit agency called Fresh Horizons to help me develop an after-school program for a difficult group of fifth graders. My goal was to address the students' deficiencies in math and reading, which prevented them from attaining a passing grade on the State's proficiency exam. Ideally, I also hoped that Fresh Horizons would send someone to inspire and mentor the kids in a way that I could not.

When its director, Carmen Hernandez, entered my classroom, my prayers were finally answered. At first, I was skeptical that she could relate to the kids, because she was carrying a briefcase and wearing a conservative dress suit – she looked every bit like the Kellogg MBA that she was. As a result, I expected the students to view her as a sell-out, because she wasn't "from the neighborhood."

I was stunned when Carmen began to address the class. Like other speakers we had invited to the school, she told the students that their best chance for a good future was not selling drugs, becoming an athlete, or appearing on *American Idol*. It was graduating from high school and going to college. But, unlike the other speakers, who bored the kids with statistics and scare stories, Carmen connected being smart and getting good grades with the very success that their idols had attained. She also gave the students some much-needed food for thought.

First, Carmen asked the students if they wanted to make millions of dollars like Oprah Winfrey or Tyra Banks. Everyone said yes. Then, she asked them how they planned to keep the vast amounts of money they would earn – and pay for the big house, sharp looking car, and other trappings of success. No one had an answer. Carmen proceeded to explain the missing piece of the puzzle that the students had never considered. In order to keep their money and take care of their families, they had to be able to grow, invest, and protect their earnings. They also needed to understand the tax forms that their high priced accountants would ask them to sign – and that required math skills.

Carmen also explained the importance of speaking proper English in order to move ahead. Learning to speak and write persuasively – and reading classics like Shakespeare – wasn't "selling out." It was developing an understanding and respect for the language and history that we all share. As an added bonus, their ability to communicate effectively would also make a positive impression on their future clients and employers, who would determine the size and consistency of their earnings. The kids had never considered that, either.

Carmen also showed compassion for a girl who had lost hope, because her parents had been killed by gang violence. This troubled child, who was living in a homeless shelter with her elderly grandmother, resented Carmen for trying to sell her a childish fantasy. Carmen sat the girl down and explained that education could change any situation, if the student was willing to learn. In subsequent weeks, Carmen tutored the girl in difficult subjects. She believed in her when no one else did. The girl now has a perfect A average in all of her classes. In my entire career, I have never seen a more profound transformation.

The world needs more leaders like Carmen, who devote their free time to the neighborhoods they came from. As a teenager, Carmen faced many of the same battles that my students face today. Yet she somehow escaped the temptations and cared enough about the next generation to come back. In my talks with Carmen, I discovered her interest in becoming an attorney and shaping our educational policy, to ensure that disadvantaged children have the resources they need to succeed. Without this intervention, many will fall through the cracks and succumb to the dead-end distractions of drugs and gangs.

The future depends on people like Carmen, who share my belief that we can win this battle and make a difference in children's lives. Down the road, I am excited to think about the many things that Carmen can do after she graduates from law school. The world, and the classroom, will be a far better place for kids.

<u>Our Assessment</u>: Many candidates work for non-profit organizations like Fresh Horizons, but few have ever presented a more compelling recommendation letter that confirms their contribution in such an honest and direct way. This letter, which came right from the author's heart, told a simple story about the way that Carmen interacted with the children and the dramatic impact it had on their lives. By doing so, the author differentiated the candidate from dozens of others with similar credentials.

Chapter 11: Letters for Older and Non-Traditional Candidates

Although most law school applicants are recent college graduates, some have significant experience in their respective fields of study. For these candidates, a powerful letter of recommendation, which highlights their maturity, focus, and professional track record, is an essential part of the application package.

In most respects, reference letters for older and non-traditional candidates are no different than those for other applicants – they should be written and organized in the same way that we described in Chapters 6 – 9. For older candidates, this is a golden opportunity to update the committee on what you have accomplished since you graduated from college. Your reference letters should explain the type and extent of your professional experiences and how they have influenced your goals. Ideally, your supervisor can provide considerable insight into your career progression, including the cultivation of previously unknown talents and skills.

Additionally, the committee will may wonder why the candidate is seeking a law degree after working for many years in another profession. If the author can provide this insight as part of his/her letter, it can complement and reinforce the material in the candidate's personal statement. Ideally, the letter will also confirm the candidate's personal and professional fit for a legal career.

Otherwise, the letter should adhere to the same principles we have reiterated throughout this publication. It should:

1. Describe the author's relationship with the candidate
2. Highlight the academic, professional, and personal strengths that the writer has personally observed
3. Support every claim with an example or anecdote
4. Compare the candidate to others in his/her peer group

Here are several recommendation letters for law school candidates who have already worked for several years in another profession. To protect the privacy of the writer and applicant, the names of all people, classes, schools, places, and companies have been changed.

Letter #26: Older and Non-Traditional Candidate

I have been privileged to know Jason Scott for nearly five years. I first met Jason when he visited my office to discuss an ethical concern regarding land development in unincorporated York County. As a State Senator, I often meet with citizens who have a vested interest in the future of our county, yet few have championed a cause as fervently as Jason.

As a lifelong resident of King's Center, Jason was a close friend of Cyrus Wright, who owned a 300-acre spread of wetlands, ponds and natural wildlife in historic York County. Before his death, Mr. Wright transferred legal ownership of the property to his children with the understanding that it would "not be developed." Just a few months after Mr. Wright's death, several surveyors and building contractors tried to negotiate a development deal with his children. To Jason's horror, the non-development clause had never been put into writing, which left the heirs free to dispose of the property as they saw fit. Sadly, it did not appear that their father's wishes were a high priority to the Wright children. When the developers made a large cash offer, the heirs retained an attorney to help them close the deal.

The proposed development, which included a gas station, two strip malls, and a 50-unit apartment building, was both a blessing and a curse to the King's Center community. On one hand, the project would bring much-needed jobs, along with two upscale shopping centers. On the other hand, the ecological ramifications of the proposed development were staggering. Thousands of migrating geese would lose their habitat, which was federally protected by the United States Fish and Wildlife Service. In addition, the proposed environmental changes would threaten the endangered species of bog turtles that are indigenous to our area. Few would likely survive.

When he visited my office, Jason's concern was protecting the survival of the indigenous wildlife. At my suggestion, he began an aggressive grassroots campaign to fight the development. Through pictures and testimonials, he documented the existence of the turtles to various state and federal organizations. Jason also displayed the photographs on his web site, which he promoted heavily on local radio stations. At town meetings, Jason took the initiative to educate the public about the devastating impact the development would have on our ecosystem. With the support of his friends and neighbors, Jason did everything possible to retain the land's ecological bounty.

Within a matter of weeks, Jason's work attracted the interest of several regulatory agencies. His preliminary data sparked a subsequent study by the US Fish and Wildlife Service, which protected the area to ensure the survival of the turtles. Largely thanks to Jason's efforts, the development deal was squashed, which left the 300 acres as a source of natural beauty for York County citizens.

Without Jason's initiative, the battle would have been lost. I applaud his efforts, not just as a public servant, but as an environmentalist and friend. Jason proved to the community (and himself) that a single person can make a significant difference in the town's future. His success in thwarting the development no doubt inspired his aspirations to pursue a career in government. There is no one better suited for the job.

Following law school, Jason can use his passion and skills to infuse the local political system with a much-needed sense of balance in making decisions that affect the community. As a State Senator in a rapidly-growing area, I've watched the community struggle with difficult issues related to land consumption, rising taxes, historical preservation, and the economic incentive of real estate developers. Although one person cannot change the world, an informed advocate can educate the public about the long-term ramifications of community growth. Jason is just the man to assume that challenge.

Our Assessment: This is a terrific example of a strong recommendation letter that was written by a public figure. However, in this case, the applicant is 41 years old and switching careers. Older applicants are scrutinized carefully in the admissions process. Many have the maturity to handle law school, but not the stamina or academic rigor. This author couldn't comment on Jason's academic strengths, but he documented his ongoing commitment to public service. Coupled with his sterling description of the candidate's personality, the committee was convinced of Jason's sincerity and dedication.

Letter #27:   Older and Non-Traditional Candidate

I am pleased to write a reference letter to support Jai Lin Wong's application to law school.

Jai Lin was the top student in three of my biochemistry classes at Temple University, where I am the Director of the Biotechnology Program. As an educator, I derive tremendous satisfaction from working with students who not only master the material, but are passionate about learning; they look beyond what is presented in class and ask insightful questions about the potential implications.   Jai Lin Wong is one of those rare students.

Throughout my lectures, he listened carefully and mastered many abstract concepts that other students missed. During my presentation about protein translation, Jai Lin quickly understood the underlying steps, including the transcription of nuclear DNA into messenger RNA which is used as input for translation. In subsequent discussions, he asked relevant questions about the differences between protein biosynthesis in prokaryotes and eukaryotes.   Jai Lin's aggressive give-and-take in the classroom kept me on my toes, which made teaching him particularly rewarding.

Thanks to his excellent analytical skills, Jai Lin was able to digest and analyze the information that I presented in class and use it to reach logical conclusions.   I assigned a variety of problems that required the students to demonstrate their skills in deductive reasoning, inductive reasoning, and reasoning by analogy.   Jai Lin easily shifted his method of reasoning as each problem required.   When we discussed Watson & Crick's classic experiments on DNA replication, Jai Lin was one of the few students to understand how the multiple variables in the experiments affected the hypotheses.   In the laboratory portion of the course, Jai Lin proved to be equally adept at designing experiments and testing his *own* hypotheses.

Jai Lin's homework assignments, which were written in a scholarly style, revealed his exceptional language skills. I normally assign numerous problems throughout the semester that require seven or eight hours to complete.   Despite the heavy workload, Jai Lin produced an eloquent two-page answer for each problem.   His precise, yet thorough, responses showed me that he enjoyed exploring scientific concepts in his writing.   Without exception, his work was of higher quality than that of many PhD candidates and post-docs with whom I have worked.

Jai Lin's interpersonal strengths were well-utilized in his work as a tutor and mentor.   From the very first session, he created a nurturing environment in which the students could succeed.   Jai Lin's maturity helped him to relate to older, non-traditional students like Sara, who expressed frustration about visualizing abstract events that take place on the molecular level.   Jai Lin encouraged her to re-evaluate her expectations and to savor the joy in small achievements. Once Sara became more confident, Jai Lin offered helpful suggestions to improve her study habits.   At the end of the semester, Sara told me that Jai Lin was the sole reason that she had succeeded in my class.   Jai Lin's passion for learning, along with his demonstrated ability to teach others, will inevitably serve him well as an attorney.

After a successful career in genetic research, in which he has published several papers and received three patents, Jai Lin has become fascinated with the legal aspects of the technologies he develops.   A law degree is a natural extension of that interest.   At thirty-eight, he is somewhat older than the typical law school applicant.   Nevertheless, Jai Lin is more than willing to accept the challenges that a legal education will present.

In my academic career, I have rarely met a student as bright and motivated as Jai Lin Wong.   His intellectual passion is accompanied by a gracious personality and an innate desire to make a meaningful contribution to society.   He will undoubtedly be a vibrant contributor to your program.   Please contact me at (email address) if you require additional information.

Our Assessment: This is a detailed letter that enthusiastically endorses an older candidate. This professor left no doubt in the reader's mind that Jai Lin was a sincere and dedicated man with much to offer the profession.

Letter #28:   Older and Non-Traditional Candidate

Please accept this letter as my enthusiastic support for my former employee, Ryan Rabinowitz.   In the fall of 2000, Ryan became a Medical Recruiter at Health Care Solutions, where I am the Senior Vice President.   Over the next five years, we worked closely on several placements for job candidates in the San Francisco Bay area.

Although it was Ryan's first job after college, he quickly made a positive impact on our company.   As a Medical Recruiter, Ryan had to decipher complicated requirements for each position and find a creative way to fill them with qualified candidates.   Thankfully, Ryan proved to be fast learner with a scrupulous attention to detail.   Many times, he worked on multiple openings with very different professional requirements.   By organizing his data about potential candidates and positions for immediate retrieval, Ryan became successful a lot faster than his peers.

I was particularly impressed by the proactive way that Ryan located qualified candidates.   In our industry, we teach our recruiters to utilize Internet User Groups as a way to connect with job seekers in the medical field.   Once he started, Ryan took the process a step further than anyone else.   He identified nearly one thousand employees of local hospitals, HMOs and PPOs and divided them by job function (physician, nurse, administrator, technician, etc.).   Then, Ryan contacted the most desirable candidates to determine their interest in changing jobs.   This simple step gave him immediate access to a pool of candidates who were "outside the radar" of our competitors. This type of creative thinking and initiative are what made Ryan exceptional.

At Health Care Solutions, we pride ourselves on being a relationship-based company.   From the start, Ryan was an excellent fit for our culture.   He quickly made friends within the company and took the time to help other recruiters who were struggling with their jobs.   Ryan also represented our firm at several local, regional and statewide health fairs, where he secured several high profile accounts for Health Care Solutions.   Thanks to his gracious personality, Ryan made a positive impression on everyone he met.

Without a doubt, Ryan's greatest skill was his ability to "read" candidates and determine their fit for a particular hospital or medical center.   During an interview, he asked perceptive questions and listened carefully to the candidate's responses.   Many times, Ryan elicited important information that we would otherwise have missed.   From my experience, this type of emotional intelligence is extremely rare – and cannot easily be taught.   In Ryan's case, it allowed him to make savvy and efficient decisions about candidates, which were later verified by reference checks.

In 2003, Ryan advanced to the level of Senior Recruiter with Health Care Solutions. In this role, he filled several top-tier clinical, research, and executive positions at San Francisco Memorial Hospital, which was a highly lucrative account for us.   His exceptional performance attracted the attention of several competitive firms, including Med-U-Call, Inc., which lured him away from us in 2005 with an unbeatable compensation package.   Although I was sorry to see Ryan go, I was excited to see the mature and successful professional that he had become.   As expected, Ryan continues to excel in all aspects of medical recruiting and management, despite the downturn in the economy.

If he desired, Ryan could certainly continue his lucrative career in the recruiting field or possibly open his own company.   His goal, however, is to make the transition to the legal side of the health care profession by becoming an attorney.   The many skills that Ryan has acquired will definitely help him succeed, including his medical expertise, communication skills, and ability to thrive in an uncertain environment.   Ryan will also bring his insatiable desire to learn more about the legal aspects of health care, which he cannot accomplish in his career as a recruiter.

As the Senior Vice President of a successful recruiting firm, I like to think that I have good instincts about people – and what they can accomplish.   In all areas of evaluation, Ryan Rabinowitz consistently exceeded my expectations and set the standard of excellence for his peers.   There is no doubt in my mind that he will be an extraordinary attorney.   Please contact me at XXX-XXX-XXXX if you have any questions.

Our Assessment: At first blush, the committee did not understand why this candidate was willing to leave an extremely lucrative job to enroll in law school.   This recommendation letter, in conjunction with the candidate's personal statement, illuminated his longstanding interest in health care and the organizational skills he would bring to the program.   It also documented his impressive career trajectory in a highly competitive field, which distinguished him as a candidate.

Letter #29:   Older and Non-Traditional Candidate

I am pleased to write a letter of recommendation on behalf of Amelia Davis-Stowe, who is an extraordinary student and linguist. I have known Amelia since September of 2003 in my position as a Professor of Foreign Languages at Boston University. Beginning in the fall semester of that year, Amelia began the ambitious task of completing a triple major in Spanish, Mandarin, and Arabic, which had never been attempted at BU. In the next four years, I was privileged to watch this amazing woman complete this herculean task with excellent grades. Her performance and commitment were nothing short of extraordinary.

During her sophomore and junior years, I taught three of Amelia's classes: *Mandarin I, II, and III* (lectures plus labs). She also completed my summer class entitled *Mandarin in Business and Commerce*, which presents a formidable challenge for most students because it requires an extensive amount of reading in an abbreviated timeframe. Before the first day of class, Amelia took the initiative to read one of the required texts. As a result, she was well prepared for the volume and intensity of the material.

In subsequent weeks, Amelia proved to be an exemplary student – she arrived on time for every class and was well prepared to discuss the reading assignments with her peers.   Although many students did not grasp the nuances of Chinese laws, including the controversial "one child" policy, Amelia easily comprehended this topic because she had lived in China for most of her childhood. As a result, she brought a seasoned perspective to our discussions about humanitarian concerns, immigration issues, and intellectual property disputes.

Amelia was a gracious contributor who stated her opinions clearly and respectfully. She also listened patiently to others and kept an open mind about alternative viewpoints. More than any other student, she stayed abreast of world news, and had an impressive command of current events in Asia and the Middle East. Although morning classes are notoriously difficult in the summer, Amelia's high energy level always kept the class stimulated. She was – and remains – one of my favorite students.

In all of my classes, Amelia worked diligently to stay abreast of the material and earn top grades on my exams, which were usually in essay format.   Despite the rigid time limit, Amelia provided clear, concise, and well-organized answers to every question. She was one of the few students to meet my high standards, which I had clearly articulated at the beginning of the semester.

Amelia's performance is particularly impressive, considering that she was working 40 hours per week throughout her four years at BU. Although this exhausting schedule placed considerable demands on Amelia, who is the sole support for her elderly parents, she managed to stay on track and complete a triple major. As her professor, I applaud her dedication and tenacity, along with her willingness to create a better life for herself.

At 39, Amelia is older and more mature than the typical law school candidate. As a result, she brings a sense of confidence and purpose to her studies that few applicants possess. In class, Amelia revealed her passion for law and policy, which offer a way to preserve peace among the nations that speak Spanish, Mandarin, and Arabic. As an attorney, she hopes to find practical solutions to the many problems that we discussed in class. After getting to know Amelia as a student and person, I am certain that she will achieve her goals. I offer her my strongest - and most enthusiastic - support.

<u>Our Assessment</u>:   This distinguished professor eloquently explained the unique strengths that this "late bloomer" would bring to law school. After reading about her exceptional work ethic and language skills, the committee knew that this was a special candidate who would add significant diversity to the classroom.

Chapter 12: Letters that Explain a Gap on a Candidate's Resume

Some candidates, for various personal or professional reasons, have a gap on their resume of more than six months. In these situations, it is incredibly helpful if an objective third-party can document the candidate's activities during this "missing" period of time. Ideally, the author should be honest, but put the best possible "spin" on the gap.

If a candidate has taken time off due to illness or injury – or to take care of small children or elderly parents – there is no need to "justify" or embellish the decision. The committee understands that there are personal and family emergencies that take priority in people's lives.

However, if a candidate has been unemployed for an extended period of time – and was not busy with family responsibilities – the committee WILL expect that person to use his/her time in a constructive manner by volunteering, tutoring, or trying to launch a business. These are all admirable activities that can enhance a candidate's application, if they are documented by a well-written recommendation letter.

The letter should adhere to the same principles we have reiterated throughout this publication. It should:

1. Describe the author's relationship with the candidate
2. Highlight the academic, professional, and personal strengths that the writer has personally observed
3. Support every claim with an example or anecdote
4. Compare the candidate to others in his/her peer group

Here are several recommendation letters for law school candidates who had a gap on their resume. To protect the privacy of the writer and applicant, the names of all people, classes, schools, places, and companies have been changed.

Letter #30:   Explains Time Off from Work or School

As her faculty advisor at Cornell University, I quickly discovered that Melissa Stone was an intelligent young woman with great ambition and an engaging personality. Her impressive achievements in the classroom made her a popular and respected student on campus. Yet few of her peers or faculty members know of the struggle that Melissa has endured during the last two years, which have made her a stronger person with a passion to help others.

With little advance warning, her younger brother died of AIDS in early 2008. Although Melissa's family had known of his diagnosis, they were emotionally unprepared for his death. At first, Melissa accepted the news stoically and refused to acknowledge her own grief.   She opted to keep the news private, rather than share it with the Cornell community. As the lone faculty member to know the circumstances of Chris's death, I was simultaneously honored and shaken. Although I treasured the trust that Melissa had placed in me, I questioned whether I could provide adequate support to her during such a devastating time.

Amazingly, Melissa completed the spring semester with a 3.8 GPA and promised to return in the fall. Over the summer, however, she decided to delay her return for a full year in order to process her grief. Melissa's motivation was anything but self-indulgent; within a month of Chris's death, she joined a program at her local hospice designed to promote AIDS awareness in the community. During her year off from Cornell, Melissa presented over one hundred seminars on AIDS prevention to local schools, women's groups, and clinics across New York City.

Upon her return to Cornell in the fall of 2009, Melissa continued to teach classes and train new participants in the AIDS awareness program. During the past year, she has been a visible advocate for AIDS prevention in New York City. To my delight, Melissa's year off gave her an increased appreciation of life and its wondrous opportunities. In that spirit, she has re-directed her professional goals to an entirely new area. Before her brother's death, Melissa was on track for a career in marketing and advertising. After her return to Cornell, she committed herself to a legal career, with an eye toward public service.

During her absence from campus, Melissa became well acquainted with several AIDS advocates in New York City. She was horrified by the shabby treatment that many patients received, either because of insurance restrictions or the stigma of their illness.   She is committed to fighting their cause. In many ways, her commitment is a way to honor Chris's legacy, to provide a voice for patients whose needs are not being met. I have no doubt that Melissa will tackle law school with the same style and grace that she brings to everything else she does.

As you peruse Melissa's law school application, you will see her grades and LSAT scores, her numerous awards and accolades, but nothing about her greatest accomplishment of all; she transformed a devastating loss into a way to help others. I desperately wanted to relate this episode, because it characterizes what this remarkable young woman is all about.

As she graduates from Cornell, I am incredibly sad to see Melissa go, but I am certain that she is destined to achieve great things.   She is intelligent, curious and driven.   She is kind, determined and strong.   Melissa is everything a law school could possibly desire.   Grab her while you can!

<u>Our Assessment</u>:   This letter captures the human aspects of the candidate in a highly articulate way.   In addition to documenting Melissa's academic record, the letter also provides a valid explanation for her time off from school. By discussing Melissa's volunteer work on behalf of AIDS, the author conveyed the young woman's exemplary character and dedication.   The committee had a greater understanding of who Melissa was and what she hoped to accomplish in the future.

Letter #31:   Explains Time Off from Work or School

For the past four years, Ana Giron has worked as an investigative reporter at WKBW television, where I am the Station Manager. With her background as a legal assistant, Ana carved out a niche doing monthly legal segments about landlord problems, noisy neighbors, botched home repairs, and appliances that are "lemons." Ana was not only the reporter, but the executive producer, for the pieces - she visited the businesses, conducted the interviews, and determined the appropriate focus for the stories. If justified, she also reported the incident to the appropriate regulatory agency (the police or state attorney's office). Thanks to audience demand, our segments quickly became weekly, rather than monthly, features.

Ana is a hard-working journalist with fine investigative techniques. She never accepts information at face value, preferring to validate every source independently. By far, her best work has been on the legal segments. In the past year, Ana aired an investigative series on "bad" doctors in Dallas, which exposed the sneaky and underhanded techniques that physicians use to hide their legal problems in other states to gain licensure in Texas. She reported several sad cases in which patients died after being treated by these incompetent physicians. In honor of her work, Ana and WKBW were awarded the 2009 Emmy for Outstanding Investigative Reporting.

Long after the series ended, Ana continued to help several of the people she had befriended. For two families, she paid for funerals and arranged for the survivors to receive free mental health counseling.   On her own time and initiative, Ana held fundraisers to help several families find better treatment for their loved ones at accredited facilities. She also continues to visit several patients in Irving, who consider her their "angel." Yet, even now, Ana does not publicize her efforts – instead, she prefers to be a silent benefactor.

Ana's success is particularly impressive considering she has only been in the United States for five years.   She moved to Los Angeles from Brazil in 2005, not knowing a word of English. With aggressive studying, she became fluent enough to work on-air within one year. I have never regretted giving her the opportunity. Ana has an excellent rapport with people of all races, cultures, and socioeconomic groups, which greatly enhances her investigations.   Viewers acknowledge her sincerity in keeping the community safe.

My reaction to Ana's request to write this letter is bittersweet, as her acceptance to law school will interrupt her career as a newsperson. Although I hate to lose one of my best people, I respect her desire to take her life in a new direction. Ana's combination of professional and interpersonal talents is rare in this industry - she understands the news and is connected to the needs of her audience. She is also exceptionally self-aware, particularly regarding her own strengths. I am confident that Ana will bring the same tenacity and graciousness to law school that she brings to journalism.

Our assessment: In a short space, this author documented Ana's professional strengths, including her considerable achievements as a news reporter. He also highlighted her skills as an investigator who is fluent in several languages. Although the author is not an attorney, his glowing endorsement of Ana's strengths confirmed that she was far more than a "talking head" who reads the news from a teleprompter.   By citing Ana's devotion to her community, he gave her application a tangible boost.

Letter #32: Explains Time Off from Work or School

I have known Jenna Wallace for six years as a volunteer and friend. For the past three years, we have served as Co-Presidents of the Orlando chapter of Kaitlyn's Friends, which offers free services and educational programs for cancer patients, survivors and their families. Jenna's talents as a manager and fundraiser have dramatically enhanced our success at all levels of the organization. I have no doubt that she will be an exceptional attorney following her graduation from law school.

Jenna's greatest talent is fundraising on behalf of cancer research. Like many volunteers, her inspiration comes directly from the heart. As a child, she lost her mother to ovarian cancer when she was just thirty-six years old. After Jenna worked through her grief, she became determined to learn as much as possible about cancer. Ultimately, she opted to pursue a career as a public health advocate in the Orlando community.

Between 2005 and 2008, Jenna raised over $6 million for the Orlando chapter of Kaitlyn's Friends, which funded an additional wing of our Washington Street facility. In addition to our original array of educational and support services, we can now offer free respite services for all caregivers who are enrolled in our hospice program. Jenna also negotiated a reduced contracting fee for our Washington Street renovation, which created three rooms for out-of-town guests who cannot afford to pay for lodging. Without Jenna's aggressive fundraising efforts, these improvements would not have been possible.

In late 2007, Jenna organized a gala benefit on behalf of Orlando Oncology Associates, which offers free and reduced price services for indigent and uninsured patients. She also volunteers at the center, where she draws blood, conducts lab tests and provides emotional support to chemotherapy patients. Thanks to her early experiences as a caregiver, Jenna understands the challenges that patients endure on their uneasy road to recovery. She is a kind and compassionate friend to all who enter our doors.

In early 2008, Jenna faced a formidable challenge when she was diagnosed with breast cancer. After our initial shock, we feared that the disease might end (or at least diminish) her ability to work for our group. Thankfully, Jenna's illness enhanced her commitment as a volunteer; she returned to Kaitlyn's Friends after a one-year leave of absence. As she recovered from her illness, Jenna came to grips with two profound revelations; (1) that breast cancer awareness must be a cornerstone of our services, and (2) that she wanted to become an attorney to champion women's health care issues.

Jenna is particularly committed to helping patients who do not have health insurance. In her role as a public health advocate, she has repeatedly lobbied Congress about the alarming statistics concerning uninsured women, who are significantly more likely to have non-diagnosed cases of breast, lung, colon, uterine, and ovarian cancer. Within her lifetime, Jenna hopes to champion a more compassionate health care system, in which the needs of the patients are a higher priority than the financial compensation of the providers. After seeing her in action, I am confident that Jenna will succeed.

From my experience, Jenna is the smartest, kindest, most determined woman I know. She is truly the best that our community has to offer.

<u>Our Assessment</u>: This letter documents Jenna's impressive ability to survive a tragedy and find meaning in her pain. The committee was deeply moved by her personal story, along with her continual commitment to help other women who suffer from the same disease. Additionally, Jenna's work as a community advocate was a great fit for the program in which she eventually enrolled.

Letter #33: Explains Time Off from Work or School

      I am proud to recommend Veronica Stone for consideration to law school. Veronica is a highly intelligent and perceptive young woman who came to Princeton to study clinical depression in rural women and children. The project was an extension of her previous research at the University of Beijing, where she published the landmark 1999 paper on the actual vs. published rates of clinical depression in children. Although many European universities subsequently offered her graduate support, Veronica chose Princeton because of our close proximity to the Clark Research Institute in New York City. We were honored to admit Veronica, as she brought compelling credentials as a scholar to our institution.

      We initially expected Veronica to join our program in September of 2001, but her plans were unexpectedly altered by the 9/11 terrorist attacks. With no advance warning, the US State Department declined to issue student visas to candidates from 96 countries, including China. To our horror, Veronica's paperwork was tied up for nearly a year until the US government implemented the appropriate security regulations for student visas. During that time, we held Veronica's position open, as she was our first choice to receive the Marie Bettencourt Memorial Fellowship. After the travel ban was lifted, we were delighted to finally have Veronica on our campus for the Fall, 2002 semester.

      In just two years, Veronica completed an impressive national study on the occurrence of clinical depression in rural areas. On several occasions, she worked with local women's and children's groups to develop and implement effective educational programs in local schools. When asked, Veronica traveled at her own expense to give lectures and training seminars to willing participants. I was amazed by the amount and quality of data that Veronica amassed in such a short period of time.

      Veronica will graduate this spring with a Doctoral degree in Clinical Psychology. She has a perfect 4.0 grade point average, although she consistently took the most demanding courses. During her time at Princeton, Veronica has published six articles in peer-reviewed journals and is completing three other manuscripts for future review. She has presented her work at four national seminars, including the prestigious National Psychological Symposium, which honored her as their 2006 Researcher of the Year. Veronica is, without question, the most dynamic and successful researcher I have worked with in my forty-year career.

      During her time at our institution, Veronica has also demonstrated her skills as an advocate and publicist. In conjunction with her work on mental health education, she wrote the text for several book chapters, along with informational brochures for parents, alumni, and potential donors. Thanks to Veronica's eloquence, she has received numerous financial contributions and interview requests from the media. Despite her obvious potential for personal promotion, Veronica prefers to keep the focus on our work. When praised, she is quick to credit the entire team for their contribution.

      Veronica is consistent, enthusiastic, and a pleasure to work with. I highly recommend her for law school, where she can spread her excitement for mental health education throughout the legal community. Thank you for the opportunity to recommend such a special and impressive young woman.

<u>Our Assessment</u>:   This letter was written by a distinguished professor with an international reputation for his research on depression. His willingness to endorse Veronica's candidacy with such enthusiasm was a testament to her skills and character.

Chapter 13:   Letters that Document an Adversity in the Candidate's Life

Some candidates face formidable obstacles to graduate from college and apply to law school.   Due to personal events beyond their control, such as divorce, illness, language deficiencies, learning disabilities, or cultural barriers, even basic milestones are difficult to achieve.   Nevertheless, these extraordinary candidates are top performers in the classroom and work environment because of their insatiable dedication and tenacity - they have a level of focus, maturity, and resilience that sets them apart from the crowd.

Many times, candidates will discuss these obstacles in their personal statements, both to share their background with the committee and to document their problems with the LSAT.   Unfortunately, in a large applicant pool, it is often difficult to distinguish genuine hardships from ordinary excuses.   From our experience, the information will carry far more weight if it is confirmed in a recommendation letter from an objective third party who has no vested interest in the admissions decision.

Although these issues are private – and deeply difficult to talk about – the way a candidate deals with them is an indication of his/her character.   If you have the applicant's permission to mention the issue – and you are willing to do so – you can provide the committee with insight into the candidate's life that they never could have acquired any other way.

The letter should adhere to the same principles we have reiterated throughout this publication.   It should:

1. Describe the author's relationship with the candidate
2. Highlight the academic, professional, and personal strengths that the writer has personally observed
3. Support every claim with an example or anecdote
4. Compare the candidate to others in his/her peer group

Here are several recommendation letters for law school candidates who have survived an obstacle or setback. To protect the privacy of the writer and applicant, the names of all people, classes, schools, places, and companies have been changed.

Letter #34:   Candidate with Learning Disabilities

I am honored to write a reference letter to support Miguel Sanchez's application to law school. As an Associate Professor of History at George Washington University (GWU), I taught Miguel in three classes before I became his senior thesis advisor. In this capacity, I spent the better part of an academic year working closely with him on a project that revealed his phenomenal strengths as a writer and investigator.

In our first class together, "The History of Gender Roles in America," Miguel wrote with extraordinary insight on a number of exam topics. In the summer of 2007, I was sufficiently impressed to hire Miguel as a Research Assistant for a project that investigated the evolution of women's suffrage in America. Miguel did a superb job of collecting and analyzing materials for me, including several unpublished legislative reports from the 1890's, which suggested that Massachusetts residents were actually quite progressive on various women's issues. To follow this intriguing lead, Miguel decided to write his senior thesis on the suffrage movement in New England. I applauded his choice both for its originality and level of difficulty. In hindsight, I cannot remember another student being willing to tackle something even remotely as ambitious.

As soon as he began his work, Miguel encountered an unexpected obstacle; the Massachusetts Historical Society refused to release certain documents that he needed to complete his study. Although most decisions of this nature are non-negotiable, Miguel refused to give up. Employing a rare combination of diligence and diplomacy, he petitioned the Society to release the specific documents that he needed for his work. In a persuasive letter, Miguel explained the historical value of the research and the new light that it would shed on a misunderstood period of American history. He also explained his particular interest in the topic, drawing parallels between the evolution of women's rights in Massachusetts and in his native Guatemala. By taking a sincere and passionate approach, Miguel convinced Dr. Emily Harris, the Director of the Society, to release the documents and discuss their relevance with him.

Miguel's undergraduate thesis was the best I have ever seen. Although he was working in a relatively unexplored area, he made convincing conjectures about the motives of the legislators and their subsequent efforts to promote gender equality in Massachusetts. His thesis was also highly ambitious, requiring a large amount of original research and an ability to create an accurate picture of history from conflicting pieces of data. From my perspective, Miguel's writing was better than that of most graduate students I supervise. Most impressively, Miguel did not allow his own biases or expectations to cloud his judgment. This skill will inevitably serve him well in the legal profession.

In my career as an educator, I have worked closely with several successful law school applicants. I would rank Miguel in the top 10% of that group. His only weakness is a disappointing LSAT score, which is a consequence of his lifelong struggle with learning disabilities. Twenty years ago, Miguel was diagnosed with dyslexia and ADHD, which impair his ability to do well on standardized tests. Rather than request special accommodations for the exam, Miguel took the test under standard conditions. In fact, for philosophical reasons, he has never requested special accommodations for any of his classes at GWU. Although I wish that Miguel had scored higher on the LSAT, I respect his decision to keep the focus on his talents, rather than his limitations. On the surface, Miguel's score may not seem particularly impressive, but it actually holds deeper meaning; it proves that Miguel can perform at parity with other candidates under extremely stressful circumstances. What more can you ask from a candidate?

Miguel is not just an exceptional student, but a kind, hardworking, balanced young man with a zest for everything that life has to offer. Our department is infinitely richer for his having worked in it.   I recommend Miguel without reservation for your program.

Our Assessment: This letter was written by a well-known professor at GWU who rarely writes such glowing letters of recommendation. Automatically, the committee knew that this young man must be something special. The letter's strength is that the author knows the applicant well and is favorably impressed by his work. The writer did a great job of citing specific examples of Miguel's diligence and research skills. By mentioning the learning disabilities at the END of the letter, he kept the focus on what the candidate could do, rather than on his deficiencies. By doing so, he distinguished Miguel from the hundreds of other applicants with disappointing LSAT scores.

Letter #35: Overcoming an Obstacle (Dual JD/MBA Program)

I am pleased to write a letter of recommendation on behalf of Ms. Regina Rogers, who has applied for admission to the JD/MBA program at Northwestern University. I have known Regina since September of 2006, when she enrolled in my course entitled Advanced Oncology: Theory and Practice at Harvard Medical School. Based on her extraordinary performance, I am confident that Regina has the requisite intelligence and drive to succeed in a rigorous JD/MBA program.

From our first class meeting, Regina demonstrated her superior intelligence and work ethic. She followed my lectures closely and asked insightful questions about the material. When I assigned outside reading, Regina immediately completed the assignments and discussed their relevance in class. By doing so, she revealed her outstanding command of cellular biology, on both a theoretical and practical basis.

On several occasions, Regina attended my review sessions to ensure that she understood the material - it is, after all, one of the toughest courses in the entire MD program. Regina was one of the few students who received an A in the class, after earning nearly perfect scores on all of her exams. Based on her interest and competence, I suggested that Regina tutor another student who was struggling in the course. With her nurturing personality and impressive command of the material, I couldn't imagine anyone better suited to help him.

In my long career, I have rarely taken the time to write a recommendation on behalf of a student. Regina is that rare exception. Her performance in the MD program at Harvard is particularly noteworthy, because she is an Army veteran who lost both of her legs during a combat mission in Desert Storm. Rest assured, although Ms. Rogers cannot walk, and is in fact confined to a wheelchair, she refuses to identify herself as disabled. Instead, she focuses strictly on what she *can* do, which is nothing short of extraordinary.

Regina is an excellent student, a compassionate clinician, and a seasoned researcher who has won several awards and published numerous papers in peer-reviewed journals. Regina is also an insightful physician-scientist with a continual passion to learn more, know more, and do more. As a result, she is a valuable asset to whatever project she joins.

Based on my interactions with her, I am confident that Regina will excel in all aspects of the JD/MBA program. With her rare combination of personal and professional attributes – including her unparalleled motivation - she will undoubtedly succeed at whatever she decides to do.

I offer Regina my strongest recommendation. Please contact me at XXX-XXX-XXXX or at email address if you would like additional information.

Our Assessment: This author is a distinguished physician who rarely writes letters of recommendation. His willingness to endorse Regina was a testament to her character and achievements. Most impressively, this author did not make the candidate's physical limitations the focus of the letter – or use them as an excuse for anything. Instead, he focused on her strengths - and what she *could* do – which made an indelible impression on the committee.

Letter #36:   Overcoming an Obstacle

I have known Mrs. Luan Lee for three years in my role as Associate Professor of Psychology at the University of Vermont.   During this time, Luan has completed considerable work under my direction, including two courses in Abnormal Psychology, a three-credit Research Practicum and her Senior Thesis.   Luan has also served as my Research Assistant for a project on women's health.   As a student and researcher, Luan has consistently demonstrated the following strengths:

1. Academic Excellence.   My advanced courses in Abnormal Psychology require considerable reading in various textbooks and peer-reviewed journals; they also require students to write a comprehensive term paper that goes beyond the scope of the source material.   Both semesters, Luan displayed a remarkable ability to stay abreast of the assignments and comprehend the subtle details of each article.   In class, Luan discussed the reading intelligently and related the information back to earlier topics. She was unquestionably one of the brightest students in the class.

2. Research Skills.   During her Research Practicum, Luan completed an impressive literature review that investigated the barriers to health care delivery in minority populations.   To do so, she analyzed dozens of relevant studies and presented the essential details of each one in her final report.   Later, for her Senior Thesis, Luan conducted individual research on the availability of health care in an inner city neighborhood in Boston.   Her paper was one of the best I have ever seen.

Based on her exemplary performance, I selected Luan as my Research Assistant for a National Institutes of Health project to improve the delivery of prenatal care for minority women.   As part of this endeavor, Luan collaborated with professors and physicians from twelve other U.S. colleges and universities.   Thus far, the quality of her work has been excellent; our preliminary results will soon be published in *Lancet.*

3. Time Management.   Luan's achievements are particularly impressive, considering the competing demands on her time.   When she began her second semester of Abnormal Psychology, Luan had just given birth to her first child.   Nevertheless, she attended every class and completed all of her work in an exemplary manner, without any delays or excuses.   During her Research Practicum, Luan was taking care of her son, going to school full-time, and collecting data at several local women's clinics.   She somehow kept up this incredible pace for an entire year, without complaining or falling behind.   As her professor and supervisor, I was deeply impressed by Luan's ability to conduct quality research and maintain an outstanding performance in her classes, in addition to her many responsibilities at home.   I have rarely met anyone with comparable organizational and planning skills.

4. Compassion & Perseverance.   Throughout her life, Luan has displayed an uncommon level of grace and perseverance.   At age six, she lost both of her parents in an auto accident in China.   Later, after years in an orphanage, Luan faced the daunting challenge of adapting to life in the U.S., where her adoptive parents lived.   Thankfully, Luan was an excellent student who quickly became fluent in English.   She has also been extremely loving and loyal to her adoptive parents.   In the spring of 2008, Luan made an extraordinary gesture when she became the primary caregiver for her mother, who was battling terminal cancer.   Despite the many complications in her life, including her rigorous course load and the care of a newborn, Luan provided compassionate care during her mother's final days.   I applaud her willingness to open her heart and home in such a generous manner.

As one of the few Asian students at the University of Vermont, Luan has represented our school at numerous events, including the annual Asian-American Cultural Fair in Washington, DC.   She also promotes the University to prospective students in her native China, who might not otherwise consider a college in rural New England.   Because of her rare combination of strengths, including her kind and gracious personality, Luan has become a respected role model in the Asian-American community.

5. Weakness.   Luan's only weakness is her tendency to take on too much, which does not leave her with adequate time for rest and relaxation.   When she has a spare moment, Luan tends to take care of others, rather than herself.   In the long run, I think she would benefit by striking a better balance between work and play.

Summary.   Luan is an extraordinary woman who will be an asset to any program she decides to join.   I offer her my enthusiastic support.

Our Assessment: This letter documented the candidate's exceptional performance as a student and researcher.   More importantly, it also confirmed her ability and willingness to balance these responsibilities with the demands of caring for a newborn child and an elderly parent.   After reading it, the committee realized what a motivated and effective person Luan was.

Letter #37: Overcoming an Obstacle

I am honored to support the law school application of Mr. Prakash Patel. Since 2004, Prakash has worked as a Financial Analyst in the Global Business Development Division of Citicorp, where I am a Senior Vice President. Based upon my five-year interaction with Prakash, I am confident that he will make a tangible contribution to his law school class.

Before he joined our department, Prakash completed his Bachelor of Science degree in Economics at New Delhi University, where he graduated first in his class of two-thousand students. Later, Prakash completed his Master of Science degree in International Finance, including an independent research project, at Sana'a University, which is one of the most prestigious universities in Yemen. As a result of this training, Prakash brought a comprehensive understanding of global economics to his work at Citicorp. In fact, as part of his Master's degree at Sana'a, Prakash conducted research on the development of microenterprise in Yemen under the direction of another Vice President at our firm, who was overwhelmingly impressed by his performance. Based on her recommendation, we eagerly welcomed Prakash into our group.

As part of his duties, Prakash conducts comparative research on private and public companies in India, Pakistan, Yemen, and Saudi Arabia, as well as risk analyses for various investment products. He also reviews materials for our financial advisors and helped to produce our annual reports. From the start, Prakash proved to be a smart and diligent analyst. Every week, he reads dozens of reports and gives his assessment to the group. When presented with alternative business scenarios, Prakash makes logical and insightful conclusions. He also defends his positions with great maturity, which few of his peers can do.

Prakash's speaking and writing skills are particularly impressive, considering that he had only lived in the United States for one year when he joined Citicorp. As a graduate student in Yemen, he faced continual persecution by the government for his liberal views on political, economic, and social issues. When Prakash refused to abandon his research, the government tried to imprison him for publishing conclusions that were unflattering to them. By seeking asylum in America, Prakash escaped this terrible oppression, but he faced the intimidating task of re-building his life in a country where he did not speak the language. On several occasions, Prakash and I have discussed the financial and linguistic challenges that he faced to complete his education and launch his career; his path to success has not been easy. Nevertheless, Prakash has refused to abandon his dream of pursuing a law degree in the United States.

From his first day at Citicorp, Prakash displayed an impressive level of curiosity about the global financial markets. He always looks for ways to enhance his knowledge and skills. As his boss, I am particularly impressed by Prakash's independence and initiative. When presented with a task that he has not performed before, Prakash always tries to find the solution himself rather than ask for assistance. By doing so, he found several ways to improve our performance and efficiency, such as streamlining the approval process for expenditures below a stipulated amount.

Prakash's greatest strength is his ability to handle multiple priorities. Many times, he receives emergency requests to generate a report or analyze a portfolio with little advance warning. Despite his busy schedule, Prakash always delivers precise and reliable results. He has also proved to be an excellent team player. In his free time, Prakash helped a colleague translate documents from Hindi to English. He also served as an interpreter when visitors from India came to our office for our annual meeting. By assuming these diverse responsibilities, Prakash has set an admirable standard for his peers.

With his demonstrated strengths in economics and finance, Prakash is definitely on the fast track for a senior management position at Citicorp. Nevertheless, his heart has taken him in another direction, which will enable him to use his skills to improve and protect society. I respect Prakash's decision and I am certain that he will succeed.

Our Assessment: Many times, a candidate will discuss an unusual life experience in his/her personal statement that seems too odd or extreme to be believed. In this case, the candidate had survived terrible threats from a foreign government because of the conclusions he reached during his Master's degree research project. This author, although not directly involved in the project, had sufficient credibility to document the dilemma and vouch for the candidate's sincerity. Most importantly, the author also confirmed the exceptional job Prakash did in his position at Citicorp, after living in the U.S. for less than one year.

Chapter 14: Letters that Explain Low Grades or LSAT Scores

Many times, as part of their applications, candidates will attach a separate addendum to explain a disappointing grade or LSAT score. Their hope is that the explanation will somehow compensate for a less than stellar "number" on their application. Unfortunately, at highly competitive schools, these addendums rarely make a positive impact on the admissions committee.

Why? Most explanations are convoluted and self-serving – and difficult to verify. Other times, the excuse raises more questions than it actually answers, such as an announcement that the candidate does not perform well on standardized tests. Well, law school *requires* candidates to pass dozens of standardized tests, including the granddaddy of them all – the bar exam. If you cannot handle a standardized exam, how in the world do you plan to pass the bar?

If you have a disappointing grade or LSAT score – and a legitimate explanation for it – it is FAR better to have an objective third party document it in a persuasive recommendation letter. What are legitimate explanations?

- Medical emergencies that can be documented by a physician's letter
- A serious illness or death in the immediate family
- Military commitments
- Work commitments necessitated by financial emergencies
- Your native language is not English
- You have a documented learning disability, but did not request special accommodations for the LSAT

In these cases, a well-written letter that informs the committee of the situation (without making excuses for the candidate) can greatly enhance the application. The letter should adhere to the same principles we have reiterated throughout this publication. It should:

1. Describe the author's relationship with the candidate
2. Highlight the academic, professional, and personal strengths that the writer has personally observed
3. Support every claim with an example or anecdote
4. Compare the candidate to others in his/her peer group

Here are several recommendation letters for law school candidates with disappointing grades or LSAT scores. To protect the privacy of the writer and applicant, the names of all people, classes, schools, places, and companies have been changed.

Letter #38:   Explains Poor LSAT Scores / Military Commitment

I am pleased to write a reference letter for Harold McMahon. I have known Harold for ten years in my role as the Director of Sales/Marketing at the Bon Ami Starch and Chemical Company. Harold's firm is one of our best customers – consequently, we have developed a close business relationship.

From the moment I met Harold, I was impressed by his strong motivation to succeed. Since early 2000, he has advanced in a series of managerial positions in the Processing Division at National Starch Inc., which produces polymer derivatives for the food and cosmetic industries. Despite having no sales background, Harold assumed a high-pressure sales role early in his career. In his first assignment, he was responsible for a ten-state geographical area that was clearly outside of his "comfort zone." Nevertheless, he quickly mastered the critical aspects of salesmanship, from cold calling to handling post-sales service problems. By building strong relationships with a diverse group of clients and peers, Harold significantly grew his sales territory and was promoted to a more visible division within the company.

Everyone who works with Harold is amazed by his commitment to his customers. He excels not only in making the sale, but in building a long-term relationship with his clients. Thanks to these skills, Harold has gradually and systematically improved his company's relationships with their largest and most strategic accounts.   Despite competition from foreign suppliers- and the continual pressure to reduce costs - Harold has successfully maintained his sales in a crowded market.

Harold's strong business acumen, coupled with his ability to work with all types of people, enabled him to assume additional responsibility at National Starch. In July of 2005, Harold was promoted to Senior Account Manager. In this role, he manages the firm's largest and most profitable customers ($145 million in annual sales), and has recently been tapped to grow the firm's second largest business segment, the "neutraceutical" market.

To me, Harold's most admirable trait is his commitment to serving his country. Since 2004, in addition to his management career, he has been a soldier in the US Army Reserves. In August of 2008, with just ten days notice, Harold left the comfort of his home to complete a one-year stint in Iraq. Needless to say, we missed him terribly and were delighted by his safe return. Unfortunately, Harold's unexpected deployment had a negative effect on his ability to prepare for the LSAT. After working with him for many years, I can confirm that Harold's lackluster score on the exam is by no means indicative of his ability to succeed. He took the test in September of 2009, just three days after he returned from Iraq. Under those circumstances, I am amazed that he did as well as he did.

Harold is a bright and hardworking man who embraces life's challenges with focus and enthusiasm. If given the opportunity, he will be a tremendous asset to your program. I recommend Harold without reservation.

Our Assessment: This letter eloquently captures Harold's unique strengths as a salesman, manager, and soldier. It also provided a valid explanation for his disappointing LSAT score. After re-taking the exam and scoring significantly higher, Harold was admitted to his first-choice law school.

Letter #39: Low GPA & LSAT Scores / Language Deficiency

a) Have the applicant's academic program and other relevant experience have prepared her/him for the study of law?

Nandika has been an exceptional student in the Honors Program at Syracuse University, where I am a Professor in the psychology department. Analytical by nature, she has a passionate desire to understand why people do the things they do. Nandika also has a healthy appreciation for the research behind the prevailing psychological theories. Many times, she asked me perceptive questions about the validity and reliability of the material I presented in class. In response, I offered relevant examples to better explain the concepts.

On exams, Nandika's writing was concise and articulate. In evaluating her work, I was particularly impressed by her organizational and analytical skills. Nandika consistently demonstrated the ability to draw realistic conclusions from conflicting sources of information. She achieved an A+ grade in my class (The Science of Memory), which is nearly unprecedented in my thirty years of teaching.

Throughout the semester, Nandika's personality sparked many classroom debates and brainstorming sessions. Although some of my students lacked the confidence to speak in class, Nandika loved the give-and-take that these discussions afforded. Fortunately, she is also a good listener who is willing to learn from others. This skill, combined with Nandika's creative flair, inspired the most unique class project I have ever seen: a software program that helps users improve their short-term memory. Nandika is convinced that everyone has the potential to improve their ability to recall facts and figures; the software is designed to help them do it. Nandika came up with the idea and developed the initial prototype. Inspired by its brilliance, I have used the software in several of my classes to improve my students' test scores. With the encouragement of her friends and faculty, Nandika is exploring the possibility of patenting the software as an educational tool. As her mentor, I am proud of Nandika's creative success.

b) Please comment on any other abilities which you feel might reflect the applicant's capacity to undertake legal studies, especially with respect to the above-mentioned admission policy of the Faculty of Law.

Nandika is a pleasant woman who forms productive relationships with her faculty and peers. She often helps other students with their coursework and initiates study groups on campus. Introspective by nature, Nandika also takes a passionate interest in the world around her. In her spare time, she works as an advocate for an international charity that champions the rights of women and children. Nandika also volunteers in the office of an attorney who specializes in criminal law. With her deep-rooted sense of moral and ethical responsibility, Nandika is eager to protect the victims of crime and oppression, who would not otherwise have a voice. A career as an attorney is ideally suited to her personality and goals.

Nandika's accomplishments are even more impressive considering that she is not a native speaker of English, nor has she benefitted from an ESL program. When I first met her, she had just arrived in the U.S. from Poland, where she taught herself English by working with an old set of Berlitz language tapes. Obviously, Nandika was at a distinct disadvantage during her freshman year of college, when she competed with native speakers of the language.

Fortunately, Nandika refused to give up. After a rocky start, she improved her GPA and found her niche as a psychology student. Although Nandika excelled in her upper level coursework, she struggled with her English courses and the verbal portion of the LSAT. To compensate for this deficiency, she took several elective classes in speech and also volunteered as a language tutor for new students from Poland. Eventually, with dedication, she learned to express herself with confidence, both verbally and in writing. In the past four years, her progress has been nothing short of miraculous.

By far, Nandika's greatest strengths are her commitment and motivation. Even during stressful situations, she completes her work quickly and effectively. I recommend Nandika with the greatest enthusiasm for your program.

<u>Our Assessment</u>: In addition to documenting Nandika's impressive academic strengths, including an unusual level of creativity, this letter also provides a valid explanation for the candidate's disappointing LSAT scores. Fortunately, Nandika's additional reference letters also highlighted her strong communication skills, which alleviated the committee's concerns about the issue. This letter also provides a glowing character recommendation by documenting Nandika's empathy and generosity. The reader walks away with a well-balanced perspective of who Nandika is and what she hopes to contribute to the legal profession.

Letter #40: Explains Poor Grades & Language Deficiency

I am writing this letter to give my highest possible recommendation for Mr. Mikhail Luba. In 2007, I hired Mikhail as a junior software developer at my new company, Bright Solutions. At first, I was hesitant to hire a college student with limited experience, but Mikhail won me over with his confidence and enthusiasm. I have never regretted taking a chance on him. Since 2007, Mikhail has participated in every aspect of the business, from core product development to marketing and sales. In hindsight, his entrepreneurial abilities proved to be exceptionally helpful in growing my business.

With minimal guidance, Mikhail developed my company's initial software product, which provided free shopping cart and checkout services to online vendors who sold their products on eBay. His programming was of excellent quality, which belied his lack of experience. I was most impressed by Mikhail's willingness to exceed my expectations, which were admittedly quite high. As I struggled with the challenges of my startup venture, I gave Mikhail an extremely demanding work load and I had little tolerance for mistakes. Fortunately, Mikhail was smart, fast, and motivated. On the rare occasion that he made an error, he quickly corrected it and learned from the experience.

In addition to his work as a programmer, Mikhail also designed the advertising materials that we used to market the product, including a web site that accepted direct sales. After launching the web site, Mikhail set up new client accounts over the phone and resolved numerous technical issues. To my surprise, Mikhail's technical and interpersonal skills proved to be an excellent sales tool. By promoting various enhancements and upgrades to our customers, he generated $825,000 in incremental sales. This was exceptionally impressive, considering the novelty of the product and my firm's limited presence in the market.

Mikhail's sales and presentation skills are particularly impressive because he did not grow up speaking English. When he arrived in the U.S. in 2005, Mikhail had only a cursory knowledge of the language. Although he struggled academically because of this deficiency, Mikhail never lost sight of his goals. Throughout the time I have known him, he has worked diligently to perfect his fluency, both through college classes and on-the-job experience. Even now, Mikhail carries a pocket notebook with him at all times to write down difficult words and phrases. By anyone's estimation, he has certainly succeeded. Most of our clients would be stunned to learn that Mikhail is not a native speaker of English.

Mikhail also showed tremendous poise and maturity when faced with personal setbacks. During his first year with our firm, his younger sister died from leukemia just weeks after she arrived for treatment in the US. Mikhail struggled with profound sadness as he recovered from this unexpected loss. Fortunately, he remained committed to his work and became an inspiring example for those who struggle with clinical depression. Regardless of his troubles, Mikhail's performance at work was always exceptional. I was profoundly moved by the maturity and elegance he demonstrated at such a young age.

Thanks to Mikhail's success at Bright Solutions, I recently promoted him to Director of Information Technology. In my 30 years of managing IT professionals, including 5 years in an entrepreneurial capacity, I have never seen anyone as motivated as Mikhail. With his rare combination of technical and interpersonal skills, along with his ambition to succeed, there is no limit to what this talented young man will accomplish.

Our Assessment: This letter provides a detailed explanation of Mikhail's ability to seize an opportunity and make the most of it. His skills in sales and marketing, along with his managerial strengths, allowed him to advance to a senior technical position in a short period of time. The committee was particularly impressed by his ability to master a new language without formal classes. His initiative and maturity were well-perceived in the admissions process.

Letter #41:   Explains Low Grades from a Foreign University

I am the Dean of Students at the Federal University of Sao Paolo, which is one of the largest and most prestigious universities in Brazil. Between 2005 and 2009, Mr. Antonio Vargas was one of our most diligent and successful undergraduate students. Among his many achievements, Mr. Vargas:

- Completed a dual major in Chemistry and Applied Mathematics in just four years

- Consistently scored in the top 1% of his class, which included the best science students in the nation

- Won merit scholarships that totaled $50,000 USD from Dow Chemical and Ciba-Geigy

- Served as Class President his senior year and delivered the keynote speech at his commencement exercise

- Published three research papers in the *Journal of the International Chemical Society*

- Completed a prestigious internship at Dow Chemical in the U.S. (2008), which led to a full-time job offer (and sponsorship for visa)

- Demonstrated written and oral fluency in English, Spanish and Portuguese

As Mr. Vargas's research advisor, I was deeply impressed by his intelligence and work ethic. For his degree, he investigated the use of biodegradable pesticides for fruits and vegetables, which will prevent insect infestation without leaving a residue or contaminating the water supply. Initially, Mr. Vargas faced several obstacles to achieve his seemingly incompatible objectives. Nevertheless, he remained dedicated to his work. Eventually, he developed a promising prototype that Dow Chemical is interested in patenting.

Mr. Vargas has consistently demonstrated that he is an intelligent, driven, and perceptive scientist. He was also one of the best students and researchers I have ever taught. Recently, when he requested this letter, Mr. Vargas asked me to document the difference in grading between the two university systems. Unlike schools in the U.S., the Federal University of Sao Paolo does not convert students' grades to a percentage or letter scale. We simply report the raw numbers. To put the information into perspective – and to compare individual applicants – the committee should note the "Class Ranking" at the bottom of the final page of the transcript, which reveals how Mr. Vargas's grades compared to those of his classmates - he ranked 3rd out of 1,450 students. By all measurable criteria, Mr. Vargas was one of our most successful and accomplished undergraduates.

Based on Mr. Vargas's success at our school, followed by his professional experience at Dow Chemical, I am confident that he will compete successfully at a U.S. law school. I offer him my strongest recommendation. Please contact me if you have any questions about Mr. Vargas's academic records. I will be happy to clarify any concerns you may have.

<u>Our Assessment</u>: Students from foreign universities face an additional hurdle in the admissions process. Many times, the committee is not familiar with the institution where the candidate completed his/her undergraduate studies. Other times, the grading system is different than that in the U.S., which makes it difficult to "translate" grades from one system to another.

In this case, the student was wise enough to ask the Dean of Students at his undergraduate school to explain their policy of presenting "raw" or unscaled grades on their students' transcripts; the only way to learn the "full story" about a candidate's academic performance was to view the Class Ranking. Thankfully, this candidate also obtained a top score on the LSAT, which eliminated any concern the committee had about his ability to succeed.

Chapter 15: Hall of Shame: References That Do NOT Open Doors

Throughout this book, we have offered numerous examples of terrific recommendation letters. From an admissions perspective, our discussion would not be complete unless we included a few samples of bad letters that failed to enhance the candidates' applications. Sad to say, but the letters in this chapter are typical of what we see for many law school candidates. How do applicants wind up with such lackluster references? Three possibilities come to mind:

1. The author did not know what to say, so (s)he said as little as possible.

2. The author was not particularly enthusiastic about the candidate, but did not decline his/her request for a letter.

3. The author blatantly sabotaged the candidate, for any number of reasons.

By publishing these bad letters, we hope to demonstrate the difference between a great reference letter and a mediocre one. In the admissions game, it can make the difference between acceptance and rejection.

For applicants, this chapter is compelling evidence of why you should choose your writers carefully and give them as much supporting documentation as possible. For writers, these letters are a convenient yardstick for you to use when you are asked to write a letter of recommendation. As a general rule, if you cannot be any more enthusiastic about a candidate than the authors of the letters in this chapter, you should decline the applicant's request for a letter. You are NOT helping the candidate if you are ambiguous, ambivalent, or unwilling to provide sufficient details.

Letter #42: Ambiguous Letter

Who is Julie Resnick? A high-energy young woman with a keen eye on the future. She is also a person of tremendous intelligence who has a gift for working with computers.

Julie has matured greatly over the last few years. Initially, her lack of commitment to her studies stood in the way of her personal and academic growth. Thankfully, at the end of her junior year, I witnessed a dramatic shift in Julie's ability to focus. For the first time, she produced top quality of work in all of her classes. In fact, Julie's skills in science and technology bolstered her confidence and inspired her to work harder in other areas.

In 2009, Julie started her own web design company. After researching what was required to launch a new business, she marketed her services to corporate clients in Providence. As she became more empowered, Julie became excited by the many technical courses available to her.

As an emerging computer scientist, Julie has taught herself numerous computer languages and has taken distance-learning classes through the local technology institute. Julie's career plan is to combine her love of technology law with her desire to run her own business. After completing her law degree, Julie hopes to develop her entrepreneurial skills by opening her own law firm.

The faculty at Rhode Island College believes that Julie's growth over the last twelve months has been nothing short of remarkable. Her focus and patience have enabled her to make friends; as her confidence grew, she began to contribute to class discussions. If she continues to apply herself, Julie will undoubtedly have a bright and promising future.

Our Assessment: Where do I start? I have no idea what relationship the author has with the candidate, because she fails to reveal it. As a result, I have no way of putting her comments into perspective. Second, she fails to provide any new information about Julie, other than that she used to be immature and uncommitted. Although the author seems impressed by Julie's entrepreneurial skills, she did not highlight them in any meaningful way. Even worse, she qualifies her actual recommendation in the final paragraph with a huge "if." By failing to provide any details about Julie's amazing transformation, the author missed a golden opportunity to sell her to a highly competitive law program.

Letter #43: Ambivalent Letter

Carmen Riggs is a bright and energetic young woman who has assumed numerous leadership positions at Antioch College. As her advisor in the Chemistry Department, I have been her professor in three classes, in which Carmen received "B" grades.

Compared to her peers in the department, Carmen is an above- average student. At times, she gives 100% to her studies and amazes us with her performance; other times, Carmen does not live up to her true potential. From my perspective, this may be due to maturity issues; in every respect, Carmen seems to be a late bloomer.

Despite her motivational issues, Carmen has managed to accelerate academically, taking senior level classes during her junior year. This fall, Carmen has enrolled in a graduate level course in Biochemistry, which requires substantial lab time and a significant amount of outside preparation. Thankfully, Carmen has been able to handle this new challenge in addition to her other academic commitments.

Carmen's impressive participation in the Pre-Law Club confirms her potential for success as a leader. We believe that she is "stepping up to the plate" for the next chapter in her life, and once established in law school, she will reveal the gifts that we know she possesses. We are happy to recommend her to your institution.

Our Assessment: Although filled with compliments, this letter sabotaged Carmen's chance to get into law school. The second paragraph, which describes her as "a late bloomer" and "not living up to her true potential," told the committee that Carmen was NOT a serious student. Even worse is the author's frequent use of the term "we," which implies that she is speaking not just for herself, but for her entire department. Law school is serious business; it should not be the first time that a candidate "steps to the plate" and fulfills his/her potential. Sadly, this type of ambivalence in an academic reference letter will tank even the strongest application.

Letter #44: Nothing But the Facts

Diana Jones worked for me as an Assistant Accountant at the Hilton Hotel from December of 2003 to August of 2005. During that time, she was promoted once and received two annual raises. Her performance reviews were "Above Average," noting her efficiency and organizational skills. All of her assignments, including our annual tax return, were completed on time and within expectations.

Diana left the Hilton Hotel to accept a position as a Junior Accountant at the Ramada Inn in Cambridge. We were sorry to see her go. We wish Diana all the best in the future.

Our Assessment: This letters includes positive information, but not nearly enough to make an admissions decision. By failing to discuss Diana's strengths, or relate them to the requirements of law school, the author gave the reader no reason to be enthusiastic about her. In fact, by providing such a terse letter, the author made the committee wonder what she WASN'T saying.

Letter #45:   Mild Sabotage

It is a pleasure to recommend Paul Hightower to the University of Pennsylvania Law School. An active young man with a love of the outdoors, Paul has a highly adventurous spirit. Consequently, he is excited about the prospect of enrolling in your school's unique curriculum in Environmental Law.

Paul has attended Wyatt College since his sophomore year. Over the past three years, he has developed a strong personality and a deep sense of purpose. As a high school senior, Paul was diagnosed with a learning disability that required a customized approach to studying. He transferred to Wyatt College after his freshman year, when the large state university he attended did not provide the level of support that he desired. Paul has done much better on our small, close-knit campus. Although he was often frustrated, he worked hard to master subject areas that were difficult for him. Thanks to the tireless support of his advisor, Dr. Wong, Paul was able to find his place on campus.

By completing college one semester early, Paul has cleared his schedule to participate in a one-semester program at the University of Alaska, where he will research the dioxin levels in swordfish. The data he is gathering will be used to support a university research project on environmental safety in rural food supplies. The skills that Paul is developing in data collection and management will be well-utilized in his law school studies.

I applaud Paul's willingness to participate in such a challenging venture, considering his previous problems adjusting to new situations. Thankfully, the program in Alaska is well-organized and well-supervised. By the time Paul gets to the University of Pennsylvania, he will already have several critical skills under his belt, including the ability to thrive in a large, unknown environment.

By pursuing the program in Alaska, Paul has shown us that he knows how to set a goal and see it through. His initiative has set a precedent for our school and has inspired his fellow students to set similarly high expectations. Accordingly, Paul has the potential to be a role model for others by channeling his energy into the work he loves best. I wish Paul the best in his pursuit of a legal education.

<u>Our Assessment</u>:   This letter appears to have been written by two different people: one who supports Paul, and another who thinks he is immature and incapable of handling adult responsibilities.   By mentioning his problems adapting to life situations, the author negated all of the great things he said about Paul's work in Alaska.   He repeatedly called attention to a negative, rather than cite the candidate's strengths.   As a result, the reader walks away confused about how strongly the author is endorsing Paul.

Summary

After reading this book, including 45 actual reference letters, we hope that you feel well-prepared to write (or obtain) a persuasive letter of recommendation for law school.

A Quick Summary for Candidates:

1. Ask people who know you well enough to highlight your strengths (and are willing to do so).

2. Give each author enough information to do a good job for you, including:

    a. a cover letter with the names, addresses and deadlines for all of the letters you need   (Appendix 2)
    b. the appropriate forms from each school that the writer needs to complete
    c. a summary of your "Match Points" (Appendix 4)
    d. a current copy of your resume
    e. your personal statement
    f. pre-addressed, stamped envelopes for all letters

3. Give the author enough time to write a compelling letter.

4. Follow through with each author to ensure that his/her letter reaches its destination.

5. Thank the author for his/her efforts on your behalf.

A Quick Summary for Letter Writers:

1. Meet with the candidate to determine whether you are the best person to write a reference letter on his/her behalf.

2. If you agree to write a letter, give the candidate a copy of the Reference Letter Request Form (Appendix 6), which summarizes all of the information you will need.

3. Do not begin until you have all of the requested documents.

4. Before putting pen to paper, be sure to review your organization's policy regarding letters of recommendation. Limit your comments to positive, factual observations that you have actually observed in your interactions with the applicant.

5. Follow our guidelines in Chapter 5 to write the best letter possible.

6. For additional help in writing and editing letters of recommendation, admissions essays, and personal statements, please visit www.ivyleagueadmission.com.

In the law school application process, reference letters can provide the committee with objective, third-party documentation of a candidate's strengths and skills.   A well-crafted reference letter can also explain a variety of personal circumstances (and obstacles) better than any personal statement ever could.   By harnessing the power of your recommendations, you will optimize your chances of gaining admission to the top law schools in the country. Don't miss this chance to claim your destiny!

Appendices

Appendix 1: College Dean's Evaluation Form

Appendix 2: Request for Reference Letters

Appendix 3: Sample Rating Sheet

Appendix 4: Sample Match Points

Appendix 5: Sample Thank You Note for a Reference Letter

Appendix 6: Reference Letter Request Form

Appendix 1: Law School Requirement: College Dean's Evaluation Form

Please provide the following information and give this form to the Dean of Students (Note: you must have the Dean of Students complete this form regardless of whether that person knows you.)

Your Name

Your Address

Anticipated Date of Graduation

Dean's Name

To be completed by the Dean:

1. Has the person named above been found guilty of any academic or other type of impropriety?

2. If so, please describe.

3. Has the applicant otherwise behaved in a manner consistent with the trust and responsibility expected of lawyers?

4. If yes, please explain.

5. Are there any disciplinary charges currently pending against the applicant?

6. If yes, please explain.

7. Would you recommend the applicant for admission to law school?

    I do not know the applicant well enough to answer
    Yes, very enthusiastically
    Yes, with conviction
    Yes, but with qualifications
    No, I would not recommend the applicant

Signature: _____

Appendix 2:   Request for Reference Letters

Name: Date:

Address: Phone: Email:

Dr./Mr./Mrs./Ms. _____,

I appreciate your willingness to write me a strong letter of recommendation for law school. This page summarizes the schools to which I am applying and the name(s) and address(es) of each person to whom the letter(s) should be addressed. For your convenience, I have listed the schools in the order in which the letters need to be received (the earliest deadlines are listed first).

I am enclosing several pages of supporting information:

a) A list of my Match Points, which explain how my credentials match the school's requirements
c) A current copy of my resume
d) My personal statement
e) Pre-addressed, stamped envelopes for all letters

Please let me know if you need additional information. Thank you for your support.

1) School 1:   Name and Address of School
                Name of Contact Person to Whom Letter Should be Addressed
                Date Letter Should be Mailed to School
                Additional Information / Instructions (if any)

2) School 2:   Name and Address of School
                Name of Contact Person to Whom Letter Should be Addressed
                Date Letter Should be Mailed to School
                Additional Information / Instructions (if any)

3) School 3:   Name and Address of School
                Name of Contact Person to Whom Letter Should be Addressed
                Date Letter Should be Mailed to School
                Additional Information / Instructions (if any)

If you have any questions or concerns, please contact me at the phone number and email address above. Thank you again for your support.

Appendix 3: Sample Rating Sheet

Factors: For each factor below, please indicate your opinion of this applicant's rating on that factor relative to other candidates you have observed.

Ranking Standards:

1. Exceptional, top 5%
2. Excellent, next 10%
3. Good, next 20%
4. Average, middle 30%
5. Reservation, next 30%
6. Poor, low 5%
7. No basis for judgment

Factors:

_____ **Emotional Stability:** Exhibits stable moods; performs under pressure

_____ **Interpersonal Relations:** Rapport with others; cooperation, attitude toward supervisors

_____ **Judgment:** Ability to analyze problems, common sense; decisiveness

_____ **Resourcefulness:** Originality; initiative, management of resources and time

_____ **Reliability:** Dependability; sense of responsibility, promptness; conscientiousness

_____ **Perseverance:** Stamina; endurance, psychological strength

_____ **Communication skills:** Clarity in writing and speech

_____ **Self-confidence:** Assuredness; awareness of strengths & weaknesses

_____ **Empathy:** Consideration; tact; sensitivity to the needs of others

_____ **Maturity:** Personal development; social awareness, ability to cope with life situations

_____ **Intellectual curiosity:** Desire to learn and extend beyond expectations

_____ **Scholarship:** Ability to learn, quality of study habits, native intellectual ability

_____ **Motivation:** Depth of commitment; intensity; sincerity of career choice

Evaluation Summary:

Compared to other law school applicants you know, please provide an overall evaluation of this candidate:

( ) Exceptional candidate, top 5%
( ) Excellent candidate, next 10%
( ) Good candidate, next 20%
( ) Average candidate, middle 30%
( ) Weak candidate, bottom 35%
( ) No basis for judgment

Appendix 4: Bethany Daniel's Preparation for Law School (Match Points)

My Preparation:

1) **Academic Preparation.** My academic and professional background are an excellent match for law school. I hold a BA in Chemistry from Brown University and an MS in Public Health from Harvard University. I earned a GPA of 4.0 in both programs, despite working a full-time job at the same time.

2) **Professional Experience.** I have also cultivated extensive interpersonal experience in both educational and public health environments to verify my suitability for a legal career.

As a teacher, I learned to communicate scientific concepts to non-scientists. I developed my public speaking skills and promoted myself as a scientific leader throughout the state. I enjoyed being a role model for students and getting them excited about chemistry. I valued the trust they placed in me and the long-term friendships I have made in the process.

As a public health manager, I implemented an AIDS awareness program in my community. I also develop educational booklets about disease prevention and give lectures to interested groups in the county. I supervise a group of lab technicians and am responsible for the actual testing and reporting of results. I thrive in my role as a counselor, particularly to young women and children. I am eager to pursue a career as a public health advocate.

3) **Outside Interests.** I am a tri-athlete who competes at the state, local and national levels. I also am a volunteer paramedic for the local ambulance company.

4) **Sincerity of Interest.** My interest in the law is a natural progression of my career in public health. Through my work, I have identified the need for increased funding and more pervasive programs to serve inner city patients who are at an increased risk for HIV, hepatitis and other sexually transmitted diseases. With a law degree, I will have the knowledge and skills to fill that need.

With my excellent academic background, strong interpersonal skills, and commitment to helping others, I am a great fit for this career. I am certain that I have the diligence, stamina, and emotional stability that are needed to complete a law degree. At age 30, I also possess the maturity to pursue my education with purpose and enthusiasm.

How My Credentials Match the School's Requirements:

As my major professor for my graduate degree, you supervised all aspects of my class work and clinical training. These are the experiences and strengths that I hope you will mention in your reference letter:

a. <u>Intellectual Drive</u>: completed 45 graduate hours in public health, including two courses (PH 477 and PH 555) that are normally restricted to doctoral candidates. Attained a perfect 4.0 GPA.

b. <u>Research Skills</u>: completed an independent research project on HIV transmission in Ghana; results were published in *JAMA*.

c. <u>Teaching Skills</u>: during my year in Ghana, I helped to establish a pre-school in an underserved area. During the summer of 2004, I returned to the region under the auspices of Doctors Without Borders, which helped me to expand the original curriculum.

d. <u>Communication Skills</u>: excellent speaker and writer; I have published 5 articles in peer-reviewed journals; I have presented papers at 3 national public health seminars at Harvard. During the summer of 2005, I hosted my own talk show, Healthier Lives, on public access television (Channel 1).

e. <u>Empathy & Motivation</u>: I work well with people from diverse racial and socioeconomic backgrounds. I have also assumed leadership responsibilities beyond the scope of my job, with a continual eye on developing my skills as a public health advocate.

Appendix 5: Sample Thank You Note for a Reference Letter

October 1, 2009

Lawrence Johnson, Esq.
Johnson & Taylor Legal Services
333 Island Drive
Warren, CT 02876

Dear Mr. Johnson,

Thank you for taking the time to write a recommendation letter to support my law school application. I appreciate the timeliness of your reply and the gracious compliments in your letter.

My motivation to obtain my law degree stems from the two satisfying summers that I worked at your firm. My first-hand experience with you and your staff was instrumental in my decision to pursue a career in intellectual property law. Thank you for giving me the opportunity to contribute to such challenging cases at a pivotal point in my career.

I will contact you during the admissions process to apprise you of my progress. Thank you again for the reference letter and for your kindness to me over the years. You've been an exceptional mentor and role model.

Sincerely,

Erica Page

Appendix 6: Reference Letter Request Form

Thank you for inquiring about the possibility of obtaining a reference letter from me. Please follow these steps to ensure that I can do a great job on your behalf.

Step 1: Arrange an Initial Meeting to Discuss the Letter

Please schedule a meeting with me to talk about the recommendation letter **at least four weeks before** you need it. Ask me if I would feel comfortable writing a supportive and positive recommendation for you.

When asked to provide a reference, I have to ask myself if I know you well enough to support your application for a particular graduate program. Acknowledging the importance of a top-quality endorsement, I would rather decline the request to write a reference than write a vague or mediocre one. Let's meet face-to-face to discuss whether or not I am the right person to write your letter.

Step 2: Provide All Relevant Documentation

If we agree that I should write your letter during our face-to-face meeting, please be prepared to provide the following documents:

   a. A cover sheet with the names, addresses and deadlines for all of the letters you need
   b. The appropriate forms from each school that I will need to complete
   c. A ONE-page summary of the accomplishments you want me to mention
   d. A current copy of your resume (including your awards, publications and honors)
   e. Your personal statement
   f. Pre-addressed, stamped envelopes for all letters

Also feel free to include ONE page of additional information that you feel will help me write the letter. This may include specific anecdotes and stories you want me to mention, along with additional details about projects or papers I have seen that would demonstrate your creativity, intelligence, writing abilities or technical skills.

Please type all information. You should waive your right to read the letter of recommendation, keeping in mind that I will still give you a copy for your records.

Note: I will NOT write the letter unless I have all of the documents listed above.

Step 3: Follow-up

Once I receive the documents, I will confirm an exact date that your letter will be sent. One week after the expected date of arrival, please verify that the letter has reached its destination. If the law school has NOT received the letter within 10 days, please let me know. I will send another copy.

Thank you for adhering to these guidelines.

Professor John Smith, 111 Rogers Hall, (555)-555-5555, jsmith@college.edu

www.ingramcontent.com/pod-product-compliance
Lightning Source LLC
Chambersburg PA
CBHW080252170426
43192CB00014BA/2655